The pleasure of cooking

Christine and Bernard Charetton

TELECUISINE

INTRODUCTION

Ovatio has been designed to make your life easier.

To get the most out of its skills keep it at close hand on your work top. With the help of this book you will discover that it does more than just grate carrots, blend soups and beat mayonnaise. It can also chop, finely chop, slice, mash, grind, beat, knead, mix, whisk , whip, extract juices, squeeze, etc...

Its 3 L bowl capacity enables it to knead large quantities of pastry, its blender bowl capacity to prepare generous soups... With its 5 speeds* you can choose the ideal pace to make bread or squeeze an orange... Ovatio frees you from all the long, difficult or tedious tasks and insures your success in making small and large dishes.

We have created and tried out over 80 recipes from aperitifs right through to desserts for every day or special occasions to help you get the most out of your processor. In each chapter the basic or standard recipes precede the new or more elaborate methods. And we have also given you some extra hints so that you can use your imagination to vary a lot of the recipes to create your own dishes.

* Please read the following note.

This book was made for the 5 speed and 2 speed units. In the recipes we recommend the speed to use for each operation, the first mentioned speed is for the 5 speed unit, the second one is for the 2 speed units symbolised by the ❷ mark.
For example : adjust the speed on 5 / ❷ on 2, and chop the tomatoes.

Some recipes require micro-waves. They were tested in a Moulinex Optimo oven (900 Watts) combining micro-waves and grill.

Photos : Hervé Amiard and Christian Radux
Graphic design : B L E U 🆃
Illustrations : Michèle Trumel
Translation : A.M. Payen

CONTENTS

GUIDE TO ACCESSORIES

The table below presents the range of accessories. Most of them come with your food processor but others are optional. The table is designed to help you choose the right accessory for what you need to prepare. You can be sure that whatever processor model you have chosen, once you get used to it, it will do absolutely everything. Don't forget also to consult the manual which comes with your processor. It contains precious information.

	METAL BLADE	GRATING / SLICING DISK 2 blades : fine / coarse grating	
	PLASTIC KNEADING BLADE	GRATING / SLICING DISK 2 blades : fine / thick slicing	
	MINI-CHOPPER	MAXIPRESS 3 extractor disks	
	BLENDER ATTACHMENT	CITRUS PRESS	
	WHISK ATTACHMENT or WHIPPING DISK		

GUIDE TO FUNCTIONS

CHOPPING
Meat p. 37, fish, vegetables
Fruit, cheese, dried fruit, chocolate...

BEATING • WHISKING • WHIPPING
Mayonnaise p. 6, light sauces
Egg whites p. 47
Whipped cream p. 50, chantilly

FINELY CHOPPING
SMALL QUANTITIES
Garlic, onion, mixed herbs p. 27
Ham, cooked vegetables p. 43
Bread, dried fruit p. 61

GRATING
Vegetables p. 23
Fruit, cheese

BLENDING • MASHING
Soups p. 19
Vegetable purees p. 43
Fruit compotes p. 49

SLICING
Vegetables p. 24
Fruit

BLENDING • MIXING VERY FINELY
Soups, veloutés p. 19
Drinks, milk shake
Fruit puree p. 48

MASHING • MAKING PUREES
Mashed potatoes p. 42
Vegetable purees

KNEADING
Bread dough p. 12
Shortcrust pastry p. 13
Cakes p. 59, pastries

MAKING PUREE
EXTRACTING JUICE
Vegetable purees and coulis p. 7
Fruit purees and coulis p. 48
fruit juices

MIXING
Pancake batter p. 17
Waffle, doughnut batter

SQUEEZING CITRUS FRUIT
Lemons, oranges p. 51
Grapefruit

5

Whipping

1. Mayonnnaise : pour the vinegar, the egg yolk, 1 tablespoon of oil, the mustard and the salt into the bowl. Select speed 3 / **2** speed 1 and switch on. Add the oil very slowly in thin streaks through the lid feeder tube.

2. Quickly increase the speed to 5 / **2** speed 2. Depending on models, use either the whisk attachment or the whipping disk.

COLD SAUCES

Mayonnaise

1 egg yolk
1 teaspoon mustard
150 to 200 ml oil
Salt and pepper

PREPARATION : 5 mins

Fit the whisk attachment to the food processor and add the vinegar, the egg yolk, mustard, salt and pepper and 1 tablespoon of oil. Set the speed to 3 / **2** speed 1 and switch on. Once you obtain an even mixture pour in oil through the lid feeder tube (in a thin streak). Wait until the mayonnaise has started to thicken before adding oil. Quickly increase the speed up to 5 / **2** speed 2.

▷ *Proceed in the same way with the whipping disk.*

▷ *To be sure of always getting your mayonnaise just right, take all the ingredients out of the fridge 1 hour before using them to bring them all up to the same temperature.*
Mayonnaise does not keep for more than one day, so eat it straight away.

COCKTAIL SAUCE : add 2 tablespoons of ketchup, 1 teaspoon of worcester sauce, 1 teaspoon of cognac and a few drops of tabasco sauce to the mayonnaise.

LIGHT MAYONNAISE : add 1 stiffly beaten egg white into the mayonnaise.

SAUCE VERTE : add 5 tablespoons of chopped mixed herbs (parsley, chives, tarragon, chervil...)

TARTARE SAUCE : add 1 tablespoon of capers, 4 gherkins, 1 shallot, 1 tablespoon of mixed herbs, all chopped using the metal blade in the mini-chopper.

Fresh tomato puree

500g ripe tomatoes
1 tablespoon olive oil, salt and pepper
PREPARATION : 6 mins

1. Wash and dry the tomatoes, cut them into pieces. Install the maxipress with the middle size hole blade in the processor. Switch on at speed 1 and place the tomato pieces in the lid feeder tube little by little. You will have to bring the tomatoes towards the blade once or twice during this procedure.
2. Season the obtained puree with salt and pepper. Add oil. Mix well and chill in the refrigerator. Before serving the puree you can sprinkle basil or snipped chervil, add anchovies and black chopped olives, mixed herbs and capers...

▷ *You may also transform the tomatoes into puree by using the blender goblet and the blade. To do this, peel the tomatoes and cut them into pieces. Mash them into a puree at maximum speed. If you prefer not to peel them, put the puree through a sieve to dispose of the small pieces of skin.*

Making a puree

1. Fit the maxipress with the middle size hole extractor disk. Adjust the speed on 1 and switch on. Put the tomato pieces into the lid feeder tube equipped with the tray.

2. You will probably have to bring the tomatoes towards the blade once or twice. You can process up to 500g of vegetables and fruit.

Sweet pepper puree

FOR 300G OF PUREE

2 red peppers (460g)
40g white onions, 150g tomatoes
1 little garlic clove
2 tablespoons olive oil
1 sprig of thyme, 1/2 bay leaf
Fresh basil, salt and pepper

PREPARATION : 10 mins - COOKING TIME: 20 mins

1. Peel and wash the onions. Wash the peppers, remove the stalk, halve the peppers, seed and remove the pale skin. Fit the processor with the thick slicing blade. Place the peppers and the onions upright in the lid feeder tube, select speed 4 / ❷ speed 1 and slice the ingredients.
2. Place the tomatoes in boiling water before skinning them, seed them and cut them in four. Put them in the processor fitted with the metal blade and chop coarsely.
3. Heat up the oil in a frying pan, place the peppers and onions in the pan and cook for 10 mins.

4. Peel and squash the garlic clove. Add the tomatoes, garlic, thyme, bayleaf, salt and pepper to the sweet pepper fondue. Pour in 100 ml of water, mix and leave to cook for 10 mins on a medium heat.
5. Then leave to cool and pass the preparation through the maxipress middle extractor disk. Select speed 1. Flavour with snipped basil when serving. You may also add black olives, capers...

▷ *You can also use the blender goblet to make this preparation. Eventually pass the obtained puree through a sieve.*

White cheese with herbs

FOR 4 PEOPLE

200g soft white cheese
1 teaspoon vinegar
2 tablespoons olive oil
4 sprigs of parsley
3 sprigs of tarragon
3 sprigs of chervil (or mint)
1 shallot
Salt and pepper

PREPARATION : 10 mins

1. Wash and dry the mixed herbs. Pick off the leaves (you will need about 30g). Put them in the mini-chopper bowl, adjust the speed to 5 / ❷ speed 1 and chop the herbs using the *Pulse* button. Peel the shallot, put it in the mill and chop it finely using the *Pulse* button.
2. Put the white cheese, the chopped shallot, vinegar, olive oil, mixed herbs, salt and pepper into a salad bowl. Mix well to blend the ingredients. If you appreciate spicy dishes you can add a few drops of tabasco.

Guacamole

SERVES 4 TO 6

1 small onion, 1 tomato
1 small hot chili pepper
2 ripe avocados
1 tablespoon lemon juice
2 sprigs fresh coriander (25 leaves)
Salt and pepper

PREPARATION : 10 mins

1. Peel the onion and the chili and cut into pieces. Wash and pick off the coriander leaves. Put into the processor bowl and chop for 30 secs on speed 5 / ❷ speed 2 with the metal blade.
2. Peel and remove stones from the avocados. Skin and seed the tomato, cut it into pieces and put it into the bowl with the flesh of the avocados and the lemon juice. Add salt and pepper and blend for 30 secs. Halfway through, stop the processor and scrape round the edge of the bowl with the plastic spatula to bring the mixture into the middle.

▷ *Guacamole is traditionnally served with sweetcorn galettes that you can buy from delicatessens. You can also serve it with small pieces of toast or raw vegetables.*

Prawn butter

50g shelled prawns
50g butter
A few drops lemon juice

PREPARATION : 5 mins

1. Reduce the prawns into a purée in the processor using the metal blade on speed 5 / **2** speed 2 using the *Pulse* button with quick bursts first, then continuously. Add the knobs of butter and the lemon juice. Blend until smooth. Serve on grilled canapés.

PARSLEY BUTTER : chop 3 sprigs of parsley, add 50g butter and the juice of half a lemon. Add salt and pepper. You may replace the parsley with tarragon. Serve with meat, poultry or grilled fish.

NUT AND ROQUEFORT BUTTER : chop 6 walnuts and add 50g butter cut into pieces and 50g crumbled Roquefort. Serve on grilled bread with aperitifs.

TUNA DIP : chop a small white onion with 6 stoned black olives, 130g natural tuna (drained). Then add 2 tablespoons mayonnaise, 1 teaspoon capers and 1 tablespoon lemon juice.

Cold sauces

HOT SAUCES

Tomato sauce

1 kg ripe tomatoes
1 onion
2 cloves garlic
2 tablespoons olive oil
1 bouquet garni (thyme, parsley, bayleaf)
1 tablespoon concentrated tomato purée
1 pinch of sugar
Salt, pepper

PREPARATION : 10 mins
COOKING TIME : 30 mins

1. Peel the onion and cloves of garlic. Chop them in the bowl using the metal blade at speed 5 / **2** speed 2. Put aside.
2. Put the tomatoes in boiling water before skinning them. Seed and chop coarsely in the processor using the *Pulse* button at speed 5 / **2** speed 2.
3. Heat the oil in a frying pan and fry the onion and garlic. When the onion is transparent add tomatoes, concentrated tomato purée, bouquet garni, salt, pepper and sugar. Stir in and simmer gently uncovered for 30 mins. Remove the bouquet garni and season to taste before serving.

▷ *Flavour the sauce with parsley, basil, or fresh, chisel tarragon.*

Bolognaise sauce

200g beef to chop
1 carrot
1 onion, 1 garlic clove
1 small celery stick (20g peeled)
50g lean smoked bacon
1 tablespoon olive oil
1 bouquet garni (thyme, parsley, bayleaf)
1 can peeled tomatoes (4/4)
2 teaspoons concentrated tomato purée
100ml beef stock
Salt and pepper

PREPARATION : 10 mins
COOKING TIME : 30 mins

1. Cut the meat and bacon into cubes, then chop with the metal blade at speed 5 / **2** speed 2. Put aside.
2. Peel the onion and the garlic clove. Skin the carrot and the celery and cut them into pieces. Chop them coarsely in short bursts at speed 5. Strain the tomatoes and chop them coarsely (keep the juice).
3. Heat the oil in a stewpan and cook the vegetables and the spices covered for 5 mins until golden. Add the meat mashing it with a fork, the pounded tomatoes and their juice, the concentrated tomato purée diluted in the beef stock, the bouquet garni , salt and pepper. Blend, cover and cook on a low heat during 30 mins.
4. Before serving remove the bouquet garni and season to taste. Serve with pasta.

▷ *You may flavour the sauce with parsley or snipped basil.*

Bearnaise sauce

2 shallots
100ml vinegar
2 tablespoons chopped tarragon
2 egg yolks
150g butter cut into pieces
Salt, pepper

PREPARATION : 10 mins
COOKING TIME : 10 mins

1. Melt the butter slowly in a heavy saucepan. Peel the shallots and chop in the mini-chopper set at speed 3. Put them in a small saucepan with 1 tablespoon of tarragon and add the vinegar. Bring to the boil and simmer until you are left with a tablespoon of liquid.
2. Leave to cool for a while then add the egg yolks, 2 tablespoons water, salt and pepper. Mix well and heat over a bain-marie. Leave to thicken, stirring all the time. Once thickened, transfer into the bowl and whisk at speed 3 / **2** speed 1, using the whisk attachement (or the whipping disk).
3. Add the butter bit by bit through the feeder tube until the mixture becomes smooth and creamy (2 mins). Add the rest of chopped tarragon and whisk for 10 secs at speed 5 / **2** speed 2. Keep warm over a bain-marie.

▷ *Goes perfectly with grilled meat, grilled, poached or steamcooked fish, fondue bourguignonne, ...*

GREEN PEPPERCORN BEARNAISE : replace the shallots with 2 tablespoons of ground green peppercorns.

CHORON SAUCE : add 2 pureed tomatoes to the sauce. Goes well with veal or grilled chicken.

Hollandaise sauce

2 egg yolks
1 tablespoon lemon juice
1 tablespoon cold water
150g butter
Salt and pepper

PREPARATION : 10 mins
COOKING TIME : 10 mins

1. Cut the butter into pieces and melt slowly. Put egg yolks, lemon juice and water in a small saucepan over a bain-marie or over a very low heat. Leave to thicken stirring all the time; season with salt and pepper.
2. Once the sauce has thickened transfer into the bowl and, using the whisk attachement (or the whipping disk), whisk on speed 3 / **2** speed 1, adding the melted butter little by little. Once you have a smooth texture whisk on speed 5 / **2** speed 2 for 10 secs. Season to taste and serve.

▷ *This sauce goes well with fish terrine or poached fish, asparagus, artichokes...*

SAUCE MOUSSELINE : add 50g of fresh whipped cream to the hollandaise sauce. Reheat stirring continuously. Delicious with asparagus or artichokes.

SAUCE MALTAISE : use orange juice instead of lemon and add blanched orange peel and 1 teaspoon of curaçao. Serve with asparagus.

Kneading

1. Put the flour, the yeast and the salt in the bowl. Select speed 2 / ❷ speed 1 and using the Pulse button, pulse for 6 short burts.

2. With the machine still running, pour in water through the feeder tube. Increase the speed to 5 / ❷ speed 2 and knead for 1 min. If you are making a large quantity of dough select speed 5 as soon as you begin adding water.

3. The processor capacity allows you to make up to 1.2 kg of heavy dough (bread dough, short crust pastry). If you prepare a large quantity of dough you can freeze part of it in the form of a flat ball (for easy defrosting).

BREAD, PASTRY, BATTER

White bread

— — — — — — — — — — — — — — —

FOR 2 LOAVES OR 12 ROLLS

500g high quality plain flour
1 teaspoon salt, 20g dry baker's yeast
290 to 300g warm water (32°C)

PREPARATION : 2 mins
COOKING TIME : 25 mins - STANDING TIME : 1 H

1. Blend together the yeast and 3 tablespoons of warm water (taken from the total quantity). Put the flour, the blended yeast and the salt in the processor bowl with the kneading blade, set to speed 2 / ❷ speed 1 and using the *Pulse* button, pulse for 6 short burts then with the processor still running, pour in water through the feeder tube and knead for 20 secs. Increase the speed to 5 / ❷ speed 2 and work for 1 minute until the dough is smooth and supple. The dough will soon form a ball; stop the processor twice while kneading to flatten the ball with your hand, then continue kneading.
2. Leave the dough to stand for 15 mins on a work surface dusted with flour, then quickly flatten with your hand and shape as you wish into 2 loaves or 12 rolls. Place on a baking sheet dusted with flour, cover with a clean cloth and leave to rise for 40 to 50 mins in a warm place (22 to 25°C). The dough should rise to twice its original volume, but no more. Preheat the oven at 240°C (Gas Mark 8). Make slits in the bread with a razor blade, then bake for 25 to 30 mins (20 mins. for rolls). Put a glass of water in the oven to help the crust to form.

* The yeast must never come into contact with the salt.

ROLLS : cut the dough into pieces the size of a large egg and flatten each ball. Fold the 4 sides in towards the middle like an envelope. Turn the balls over and shape them with your floured fingers.

Short crust pastry
- - - - - - - - - - - - - - - - - - -

FOR 1 FLAN CASE DIAM. 28 CM

200g flour, 100g butter
(at room temperature)
1 pinch salt, 50ml water

PREPARATION : 5 mins

1. Put the flour in the processor bowl, add the salt and butter cut into little pieces. Mix for 10 secs on speed 2 / ❷ speed 1 with the kneading blade, then pour in the water through the feeder tube with the processor still running. Knead for 15 secs on speed 4 / ❷ speed 2 to form a ball of pastry. Leave the pastry to stand for 30 mins in a cool place.

▷ *Do not knead the pastry too long as it could « toughen » during cooking.*
▷ *You can cook the pastry on its own without filling. Either prick the base and pinch down the edges with a fork or place a circle of greaseproof paper and weighed down with dry beans to stop it from rising too much.*
▷ *You can easily double the quantity of ingredients. If you do not use all the pastry, freeze it in the shape of a flat ball. This shape is easier to defrost.*
▷ *For a savoury tart you can replace the water with an egg. The pastry can support the humidity of the filling better and keeps crunchy.*
▷ *You can add a tablespoon of sugar when preparing a dessert.*

Kneading

1. Put the flour, the salt and the pieces of butter in the bowl. Select speed 2 / ❷ speed 1 and mix for 10 secs.

2. Pour water into the feeder tube with the processor still running.

3. Mix for 15 secs (depending on the quantity) an speed 4 / ❷ speed 2 until the pastry forms a ball. If you are preparing a large quantity of pastry, use speed 5 / ❷ speed 2.

Shortbread pastry

FOR 1 FLAN CASE DIAM. 28CM

200g flour
100g butter
(at room temperature)
100g caster sugar
2 egg yolks
1 pinch of salt

PREPARATION : 5 mins

1. Cut the butter into pieces and beat it with the sugar for 10 secs on speed 3 / ❷ speed 1 using the kneading blade. Add the egg yolks and knead for 10 secs until the mixture whitens. Pour in the salt and silted flour. Knead for 15 secs on speed 4 / ❷ speed 2 until the ingredients are well mixed. Remove the pastry and work it by hand into a ball. Leave to stand 1 hour in a cool place.

▷ *You can flavour the pastry with vanilla, orange blossom or cinnamon*

▷ *This pastry is perfect for fresh fruit tarts.*

SHORTBREAD BISCUITS : roll out the pastry and cut out separate biscuits with a cutter. Bake on a greased baking tin dusted with flour.

Choux pastry

FOR 16 CHOUX

200ml water
1 pinch salt
80g butter
160g flour
4 eggs (60g/65g)

PREPARATION : 10 mins

1. Put the water, salt and the butter cut into pieces into a saucepan. Bring to the boil and add sifted flour in one go. Mix briskly with a wooden spoon until a ball of dry pastry forms, making sure that it does not stick to the saucepan bottom. Leave to cool.
2. Transfer the pastry into the processor bowl. Fit the kneading blade and select speed 3 / ❷ speed 1. Switch on and add the eggs one by one through the feeder tube. Increase the speed to 4 / ❷ speed 2. Work the pastry until all the ingredients are well mixed and the pastry smooth. While working the pastry the air gets built into the mixture that is what puffs up the choux pastry. Leave to cool before handling.
3. To make choux : grease and flour a baking tray. Preheat the oven at 180°C (Gas Mark 6). Using a piping bag with a 9mm socket or 2 teaspoons pipe out well spaced dots of the mixture onto the baking tray. Brush with egg yolk mixed with very little water. Put the baking tray in the oven and bake for 20 mins, then leave in the oven for a further 5 mins with the door half open. Leave to cool on a cooling rack.

▷ *Depending on the final use, a pinch of sugar can be added.*

Profiteroles ▷

Waffle batter

FOR 14 TRADITIONAL WAFFLES

3 eggs, 80g sugar
100g melted butter
1 pinch of salt
300g flour
1 packet baking powder
1/2 litre lukewarm milk

PREPARATION : 5 mins

1. Fit the blender attachment in the processor and put the eggs, sugar, salt and melted butter into the mixing bowl. Select speed 3 / ② speed 1 and give 4 or 5 short burts (*Pulse*). Intervene once to bring the flour into the centre. Next put the milk through the lid and gradually increase the speed until you reach speed 5 / ② speed 2 to obtain a smooth mixture. Leave to stand for 30 mins.

FOR 8 LIGHT WAFFLES

2 large eggs, 60g sugar
125g flour
75g melted butter
200 ml milk
Icing sugar to serve

1. Fit the metal blade in the processor and put the egg yolks, flour and melted butter into the mixing bowl. Switch on at speed 1 and pour in the milk through the feeder tube while gradually increasing the speed to 5 / ② speed 2.
2. Leave the mixture to stand 15 mins. Wash the bowl and replace the metal blade with the whisk attachment (or whipping disk). Add the egg whites with a pinch of salt and beat to a stiff snow on speed 5 / ② speed 2. Fold the egg whites carefully into the mixture and use it straight away.

Pour some of the mixture into a hot waffle iron and start cooking the first waffles, continuing until all the mixture has been used.
Sprinkle with icing sugar before serving.

▷ *You can serve the waffles with chantilly, fruit, chocolate sauce...*

Fritter batter

FOR 25 TO 30 FRITTERS

125g flour
1 egg
1 tablespoon oil
1 pinch salt
150ml milk

PREPARATION : 5 mins

Pour all the ingredients into the processor bowl fitted with the metal blade (or into the blender goblet). Select speed 4 / ② speed 2 and blend until the mixture is smooth and of a coating consistency. Leave the batter to stand for 1 hour in the refrigerator. You can then use it as it is or add a stiffly beaten egg white.

APPLE FRITTERS : peel and slice 700g of apples coating the slices in lemon juice. Sprinkle with sugar and leave to soak while the batter is standing in the fridge. Heat up oil in a deep frying pan, immerse the slices of apple in the batter and fry them 4 by 4.

Crêpe batter

FOR 22 THIN PANCAKES

300g flour
3 eggs
1/2 litre milk
75g melted butter

PREPARATION : 5 mins

1. With blender attachment : pour the milk into
the blender, switch on speed 3 / ❷ speed 1
and pour in the eggs, flour and lastly the
melted butter. Mix to obtain a smooth texture.
Leave the batter to stand for 30 mins before
using it.
2. With the metal blade : put all the ingredients
in the processor bowl and blend on speed 4 /
❷ speed 1. You can lightly sweeten the batter
with sugar (20g) or flavour it with orange
blossom, vanilla essence, rhum, kirsch, Grand-
Marnier.

▷ Place the pancakes already made on a large
plate on top of a warm bain-marie to keep them
warm and cover with another plate.

▷ Serve the pancakes with caster sugar, jam or
stewed fruit.

▷ Sprinkle them with sugar and squeeze a few
drops of lemon. Fold the pancakes into triangles.

▷ Heat some honey or maple syrup and pour
over pancakes. Fold them in four.

▷ Put a tablespoon of chopped sweetened
strawberries in the middle of each pancake, close
like an envelope, sprinkle with icing sugar and
serve with cream.

▷ Fill the pancakes with ice-cream, fold
towards the centre and pull up in order to create
a pouch shape. Place quickly in oven before
serving with fruit sauce.

Mix

Pancake batter : pour the milk into the mixing
bowl, switch on at speed 3 / ❷ speed 1 and
add eggs, flour and lastly the melted butter.

Pancakes with maple syrup

FOR 12 SMALL PANCAKES

125g flour
1 teaspoon baking powder
1 teaspoon maple syrup
1 pinch salt
1 large egg
150ml milk at room temperature
Butter or oil for the pans

1. Fit the processor with the plastic kneading
blade : pour sifted flour and baking powder
into the bowl. Add syrup, salt, egg and milk.
Select speed 1 and start to beat. Gradually
increase the speed to 5 / ❷ speed 2 to obtain a
smooth texture. Leave to stand for 30 mins.
2. Heat the oil or butter in non-sticking pans of
12cm diameter and pour in batter using a ladle.
Cook on a medium heat until both sides are
golden. Serve with maple syrup.

SOUPS

Leek and potato soup

SERVES 4

150g peeled leeks
150g peeled potatoes
20g butter, 200ml milk
Nutmeg
2 nice sprigs of chervil
Salt, pepper

PREPARATION : 10 mins
COOKING TIME : 30 mins

1. Peel the leeks. Fit the thick slicing blade to the processor and select speed 4 / ❷ speed 1. Place the vegetables upright in the feeder tube and chop finely.
2. Melt the butter in a saucepan and add the leeks. Stir, cover and cook for 10 mins.
3. Peel the potatoes and cut them in half lengthways. Stand them upright in the feeder tube and slice them finely. When the leeks have been cooking for 10 mins, add the potatoes. Season with salt and pepper and grated nutmeg. Pour the milk and 1/2 litre hot water into the saucepan. Cook for a further 15 to 20 mins.
4. Chop the chervil in the mini-chopper, season the soup to taste and sprinkle with chervil.

▷ *You can change the flavour of the soup by using parsley, tarragon, basil...*

▷ *You may also blend the soup in the blender attachment or in the bowl using the metal blade and add a tablespoon of cream.*

Cream of tomato soup

SERVES 4

800g fresh tomatoes
1 small onion
1 clove of garlic
2 tablespoons olive oil
1 sprig thyme
2 tablespoons fresh cream
10 basil leaves
Salt, pepper

PREPARATION : 10 mins
COOKING TIME : 25 mins

1. Peel the onion and the clove of garlic. Chop them finely in the mini-chopper on speed 3. Scald the tomatoes in boiling water first and skin them, seed them and cut them into pieces. Put them into the processor bowl with the metal blade fitted in and chop roughly using short bursts *(Pulse)* on speed 5 / ❷ speed 2.
2. Heat up the oil in a saucepan, add the onion and garlic and fry on a low heat for 2 mins. Add the chopped tomatoes, thyme, salt and pepper , mix well and pour in 1/3 litre of boiling water. Leave to cook uncovered for 20 mins.
3. Remove the thyme and pour the soup into the blender attachment. Select speed 1 / ❷ speed 1 and blend. Increase the speed quickly until 5 / ❷ speed 2 and blend for 40 secs.
4. Return the blended soup to the saucepan and add the cream. Heat for 2 mins, season to taste and sprinkle with chopped basil.

▷ *For added flavour put in fresh blanched broad beans with their skins removed (remove simply by pressing between fingers).*

Vegetable soup with curry

SERVES 4

2 carrots 110g
1 small courgette 160g
1 leek
1 potato 150g
1 stick celery
1 clove garlic
20g butter
2 sprigs parsley
1/2 teaspoon of curry
Salt, pepper

PREPARATION : 10 mins
COOKING TIME : 30 mins

1. Peel and wash all the vegetables (do not peel the courgette). Fit the slicing disk on the processor, select speed 4 / ❷ speed 1 and slice the vegetables standing upright in the feeder tube.
2. Melt the butter in a large saucepan and add the vegetables and the garlic. Cook for 4 - 5 mins stirring continuously. Sprinkle the curry, season with salt and pepper and mix. Pour in 3/4 litre of very hot water. Bring to the boil and simmer for 25 mins. Chop the parsley in the mini-chopper and sprinkle over the soup just before serving.

MINESTRONE : leave out the curry and add tomatoes, green or haricot beans, 1 onion and noodles. Flavour the soup with basil.

Blending

1. You can blend up to 1 litre of soup, compote... Fit the metal blade to the processor and put the cooked vegetables into the bowl with their cooking water.

2. Set the speed on 2 / ❷ speed 1 and increase gradually to 5 / ❷ speed 2. Allow 20 to 30 secs for soup.

3. For an even texture use the blender attachment for blending and liquidizing. Set on speed 2 / ❷ peed 1 and gradually increase the speed to 5 / ❷ to 2. The removable measuring stopper allows ingredients to be added while you are already mixing.

Cream of mushroom soup

SERVES 4

130g potatoes
250g button mushrooms
25g butter
1/2 litre of chicken stock
200ml milk
1 tablespoon fresh cream
Salt, pepper

PREPARATION : 10 mins
COOKING TIME : 22 mins

1. Peel and wash vegetables. Cut the potato into pieces and chop it in the processor with the metal blade on speed 5 / ❷ speed 2 using the *Pulse* button.
2. Melt the butter in a saucepan and add the chopped potato. Stir and leave to melt while you chop the mushrooms. Add the chopped mushrooms to the contents of the saucepan, season with salt and pepper and leave to cook for 2 mins.
3. Pour in the very hot chicken stock and the milk. Cover and leave to simmer on a low heat for 20 mins. When cooked pour the soup into the blender attachment, set on speed 2 / ❷ speed 1 and blend. Gradually increase the speed to 5 / ❷ to 2 and blend for 30-40 secs. Return the soup to the saucepan, add the cream, season to taste. Mix in and reheat for 2 mins. Serve straight away.

▷ *Before serving you can add some pleurotuses or wild mushrooms fried in butter.*

Gaspacho

SERVES 6

1/2 cucumber (280g)
2 tomatoes (400 g)
1/2 green pepper
1 small mild onion
2 cloves garlic
20g stale bread
1 teaspoon wine vinegar
A few drops of tabasco sauce (optional)
2 tablespoons olive oil
1/2 lemon
Salt, pepper

PREPARATION : 20 mins

1. Peel the cucumber and seed the tomatoes, peel the green pepper, the onion and the garlic cloves. Cut all these ingredients into pieces, put them in a salad bowl and add 400ml of very cold water, the vinegar, the tabasco, salt and pepper.
2. Mince the bread for 10 secs using the blender attachment on speed 5 / ❷ speed 2, then pour in the contents of the salad bowl and blend until the mixture is smooth (50 secs). Transfer into a soup tureen and add the olive oil and 1 tablespoon of lemon juice. Mix in, season to taste and leave in the refrigerator.

▷ *You can prepare little dishes of cucumber, tomato, onion and green pepper, mixed herbs and bread cubes to accompany the soup.*

▷ *The tomatoes will be easier to skin if you scald them in boiling water for 20 secs.*

Gaspacho ▷

Chilled avocado soup

SERVES 6

2 avocados (100g, net 280g)
1 clove garlic
1/2 litre lean chicken stock
1/2 small strong pimento
1 low fat yoghurt (125g)
1 lemon
1 teaspoon freh snipped coriander
Salt, pepper

PREPARATION : 10 mins
COOKING TIME : 15 mins

1. Peel the garlic cloves. Wash the pimento. Put these ingredients into the mini-chopper and chop finely. Put the garlic and the pimento into a saucepan with the chicken stock and cook for 15 mins. Leave to cool.
2. Peel the avocados, remove the stone and cut the flesh into pieces. Put them into the blender bowl, add lemon juice and the cooled chicken stock. Add salt and pepper. Set the speed on 2 / ❷ speed 1 and start to blend. Increase the speed to 5 / ❷ speed 2 and blend until the mixture is smooth. Season to taste and refrigerate for 1 hour.
3. Before serving, whisk in the yogurt and sprinkle the snipped coriander. Serve in goblets. You can add some ice cubes to the soup.

Watercress soup

SERVES 4

1 bunch of watercress
1 leek white (peeled 80g)
2 potatoes
15g butter
1/2 litre chicken stock
100ml milk
100ml fresh cream
Salt, pepper

PREPARATION : 10 mins
COOKING TIME : 25 mins

1. Separate, wash and drain the watercress. Keep some leaves to garnish. Peel and wash the leek and the potatoes. Coarsely chop these ingredients in the processor bowl using the metal blade set on speed 5 / ❷ speed 2.
2. Melt the butter in a saucepan and add the vegetables. Cover and cook for 5 mins. Season, then add the chicken stock and the milk. Cover and cook for 20 mins.
3. Leave to cool a little, then pour the mixture into the blender set at speed 2 / ❷ speed 1 and start to blend. Increase the speed to 5 / ❷ speed 2 and blend to obtain a smooth texture. Add the cream, season to taste and re-heat for 2-3 mins. Garnish with the watercress leaves.

SALADS, STARTERS

Grated carrots

SERVES 4

300g carrots, 1 teaspoon mustard
1 teaspoon vinegar, 3 tablespoons oil
1 tablespoon chopped parsley, salt, pepper

PREPARATION : 5 mins

1. Peel and wash the carrots. Cut the carrots
into pieces 6 - 7 cm long and lay them flat in
the feeder tube. Grate the carrots using the
coarse grating blade on speed 4 / ❷ speed 1.
2. Dress with vinaigrette : dissolve the salt in
the vinegar, add the pepper and mustard, then
the oil. Add the chopped parsley at the end.

▷ *You can also use the fine grater. In this case
select speed 5 / ❷ speed 2.*
▷ *Instead of mustard add a pinch of ground
caraway and a finely chopped clove of garlic.*
▷ *Mix carrots with grated apple, use lemon
juice instead of vinegar and add some raisins
and ground hazelnuts.*

Beetroot salad

SERVES 4

2 beetroot, 1 small shallot
1 teaspoon vinegar
1 tablespoon groundnut oil
2 tablespoons sunflower oil
Chives, salt and pepper

PREPARATION : 5 mins

Peel the beetroot and stand them upright in the
feeder tube. Slice them using the thick slicing

Grating • Slicing

1. With the coarse grating blade grate carrots,
beetroot, apple and with the thick slicing blade
make thick slices. For grating or slicing select
speed 4 or 5 / ❷ speed 1or 2 depending on
the ingredients.

2. By placing the ingredients horizontally in
the feeder tube you will get long slivers or
slices. Use the pusher to push the food down
the feeder tube. You can prepare up to 1 kg of
food at a time.

blade on speed 4 / ❷ speed 1. Dress with
vinaigrette and sprinkle with scissor-snipped
chives.

▷ *Can be accompanied by lambs' lettuce,
chicory and nuts or button mushrooms.*

Grating • Slicing

1. With the fine grating blade, grate carrots, cheese... and with the thin slicing blade, slice potato, cucumber , courgettes... Select speed 5 or 4 / ❷ speed 2 or 1 depending on the ingredients.

2. By placing the ingredients vertically in the feeder tube, you will get short slivers or round slices. Use the pusher to push the food down the feeder tube. You can prepare up to 1 kg of food at a time.

Cucumber yoghurt

SERVES 4

1 cucumber
1 teaspoon vinegar
1 or 2 tablespoons olive oil
1 yoghurt
Freshly snipped mint
Salt, pepper

PREPARATION : 5 mins

Fit the thin slicing disk. Peel the skinned cucumber*, stand upright in the feeder tube and cut into round slices on speed 5 / ❷ speed 2. Season with yoghurt vinaigrette. Sprinkle with mixed herbs.

* (Remove the centre of the cucumber with a potato peeler by rotating around the seeds).

▷ *For special occasions use cream instead of yoghurt, dill instead of mint and serve with smoked fish (Salmon, halibut) marinated in lemon juice and dill.*

RAW VEGETABLE HORS D'OEUVRE : create a mixture depending on the time of the year and season with a vinaigrette or soft white cheese and herbs.

GREEK SALAD : slice cucumber, tomatoes, onion and red or green pepper in slices using the thick slicing disk. Dress with olive oil vinaigrette and serve with fresh feta cheese and olives.

Waldorf salad

SERVES 4

1/2 of a whole celery
(200g peeled)
2 Granny Smith apples
1/2 lemon
50g walnuts
1 egg yolk
1 teaspoon white mustard
100ml sunflower oil
2 sprigs parsley
Salt, pepper

PREPARATION : 10 mins

1. Peel the apples and cut into eight. Fit the thick slicing disk and select speed 4 / **2** speed 1. Put the pieces of apple upright into the feeder tube and slice. Quickly sprinkle the apple pieces with lemon juice to avoid discolouring.
2. Peel the celery and cut the sticks into long pieces. Place them upright in the feeder tube and slice.
3. Prepare a mayonnaise : fit the whisk attachment (or the whipping disk) to the processor and put in the egg yolk, mustard, 1 tablespoon of oil, salt and pepper. Mix at speed 3 / **2** speed 1. Once you have got an even mixture gradually pour the rest of the oil into the feeder tube while increasing the speed to 5 / **2** speed 2. Add 2 tablespoons of water at the end.
4. Pour the mayonnaise into a salad bowl. Add the celery, the apples, the chopped parsley and the walnuts. Mix carefully and serve very cool.

Raw vegetable hors d'œuvre

Coleslaw

SERVES 4 TO 6

300g white cabbage (net 260g)
1 stick of celery 50g (net 30g)
2 carrots (net 150g)
1 Granny Smith apple 240g
1 small onion
4 tablespoons mayonnaise
2 tablespoons single cream
1 tablespoon vinegar
1 tablespoon powdered mustard
Salt and pepper

PREPARATION : 15 mins

1. Peel and wash the cabbage, celery, onion and carrots. Peel and core the apple.
2. Fit the thick slicing disk and put the cabbage pieces into the feeder tube. Set on speed 4 / ❷ speed 1 and chop the cabbage. Do the same with the onion and the celery (Put the celery sticks in vertically).
3. Change the slicing blade for the coarse grating blade and grate the carrots and the apple on speed 4/ ❷ speed 1.
4. Put all the ingredients into a salad bowl. Mix the mayonnaise, cream, vinegar and the mustard in a bowl. Pour the mixture over the vegetables and mix carefully.

▷ *You can add coarsely chopped nuts.*

Fish terrine

SERVES 6

5 sprigs dill
2 sprigs parsley
Peel of 1/2 lemon
300g white fish fillet (sole, whiting, cod...)
250g salmon, 25g decrusted white bread
2 large eggs, 150g fresh cream
Salt and white pepper
10g butter for the terrine

PREPARATION : 20 mins
COOKING TIME : 35 mins

1. Pre-heat the oven at 180°C (Gas Mark 6). Grease a 3/4 litre terrine. Wash, dry and remove the leaves from the parsley and the dill. Chop the lemon peel finely in the mini-chopper and put aside. Clean the bowl and chop the mixed herbs (you will obtain 2 tablespoons). Remove the bones from the fish.
2. Fit the metal blade and place the bread in the processor bowl. Select speed 5 / ❷ speed 2 and chop for 15 secs. Cut the salmon and the white fish fillets into pieces and add them to the contents of the bowl. Chop again for 10 to 15 secs. Add the eggs, cream, lemon peel, salt and pepper and mix in for 10 secs at speed 3 / ❷ speed 1. Take half of this filling and spread it into the terrine.
3. Add the mixed herbs to the remainder of the filling and mix for 5 secs on speed 2 / ❷ speed 1. Then spread this on top of the first layer. Smooth evenly.
4. Cover the terrine and place it in a very hot water bain-marie for 35 mins. Serve the terrine hot with lemon butter or sorrel sauce or cold with tomato purée on a herb mayonnaise.

▷ *Use whole filleted fish or fillet them yourself. Pre-filleted fish stored on ice before being purchased release too much water during cooking.*

▷ *Sink a knife into the terrine to see if it is cooked. The knife should come out clean.*

Farmhouse paté

SERVES 6 TO 8

250g boneless pork loin
200g shoulder of veal
200g bacon fat
1 tablespoon brandy
4 sprigs parsley
150g mushrooms
1 good sized shallot
1 large egg
1 level teaspoon salt
Nutmeg, pepper
1 sprig thyme
1 bayleaf

PREPARATION : 15 mins
COOKING TIME : 1 hour 15

1. Cut the meat and the bacon fat into pieces. Fit the metal blade on the processor, put the meat and bacon fat into the bowl and chop for 10 secs on speed 5 / **2** speed 2, then give 4 to 5 bursts with the *Pulse* button. Put the meat aside in a salad bowl, add the brandy and mix.
2. Clean the mushrooms and slice them using the thick slicing blade on speed 4 / **2** speed 1. Chop the parsley and the peeled shallot in the mini-chopper for 3 secs. Add to the contents of the salad bowl. Stir in the egg and season with salt, pepper and nutmeg. Mix well.
3. Pre-heat the oven at 180°C (Gas Mark 6). Put the mixture into a 1 litre terrine and smooth evenly. Sprinkle with thyme leaves and put the bayleaf in the middle. Cover and place the terrine in a simmering bain-marie, cook in the oven for 1 hour 15. Leave the terrine to cool for at least 15 hours before serving.

Chopping small quantities

1. Use the mini-chopper to chop small quantities (up to 100g depending on the type of food). Cut a small onion or shallot into pieces and add the mixed herbs.

2. Dry the herbs well before chopping. Select speed 3 and chop for 3 secs. Do the same for fruit peel, spices or dried fruit (up to 100g). Adjust the speed from 1 to 5 according to the preparation. Use the Pulse button for best results.

Terrine of duck

SERVES 6

1 small ducking (1 kg 200)
120g fat bacon
120g veal shoulder
1 untreated orange
1 good size shallot
2 tablespoons brandy, 2 eggs
Grated nutmeg
1 pinch of ground cinnamom
1 sprig fresh thyme
Salt and pepper

PREPARATION : 20 mins
COOKING TIME : 1 hour 15

1. Wash the orange and remove the peel with a potato peeler. Chop it in the mini-chopper by pressing the *Pulse* button 6 times on speed 3. Squeeze the juice using the citrus press (speed 1). Peel and quarter the shallot.
2. Remove the skin from the duck then take the flesh off without damaging the fillets. To make it easier ask your poulterer to perform this operation. Cut the fillets in long thin straps, place them in a hollow plate and sprinkle with the blended cognac and orange juice.
3. Cut the rest of the flesh and the duck liver as well as the other meats into pieces and put them into the processor bowl. Fit the metal blade and add the shallot. Set on speed 5 / ❷ speed 2 and chop for 10 secs. Add the beaten egg, salt, pepper, the cinnamom, some grated nutmeg and half of the marinade. Mix with 4 to 5 short bursts of the *Pulse* button.
4. Preheat the oven at 160°C (Gas Mark 5 to 6). Fill a litre terrine with alternate layers of filling mixture and duck slices. Finish off with a layer of filling mixture and sprinkle the thyme. Cover and place the terrine in a bain-marie. Put into the oven and cook for 1 hour 15.
5. Leave to cool and place the terrine in the refrigerator until the next day.

Terrine of chicken liver paté

SERVES 4

250g of chicken livers
100g lean bacon
20g butter
20g decrusted white bread
3 tablespoons milk
3 tablespoons white port
80g fresh cream
1 shallot, 1 egg
Nutmeg
Salt and pepper

PREPARATION : 10 mins
COOKING TIME : 35 mins

1. Carefully clean the chicken liver. Put it into a salad bowl and sprinkle with port. Peel and chop the shallot. Dice 50g of bacon and cut the other 50g in slices. Crumb the bread and soak in the milk.
2. Melt 10g butter in a saucepan and cook the shallot. Add the diced bacon, the chicken liver and its marinade. Cook for 3 to 4 mins on a low heat.
3. Leave to cool a little then fit the metal blade on the processor and pour the mixture into the bowl. Add cream, the drained and pressed breadcrumbs, salt, pepper and some grated nutmeg. Add the egg and mix for 20 secs at speed 5 / ❷ speed 2.
4. Preheat the oven at 180° (Gas Mark 6). Grease a small 1/2 litre terrine, then pour in half of the liver paté purée mixture. Place the slices of bacon on top of this mixture then cover the bacon with the remainder of the liver purée. Cover and place the terrine in a simmering bain-marie and cook in the oven for 20 mins.
5. Remove the lid and continue to cook for 10 mins. Leave to cool and refrigerate.

Cheese soufflé

SERVES 6

10g butter to grease the dish
100g cheese (emmenthal,
cheddar or parmesan)
45g butter
30g sieved flour
375g milk
6 eggs
grated nutmeg
Salt and pepper

PREPARATION : 10 mins
COOKING TIME : 40 mins

1. Butter a Ø 21cm soufflé dish. Preheat the
oven at 200°C (Gas Mark 6 to 7). Fit the fine
grating disk on the processor. Cut the cheese in
pieces and grate it at speed 4 / ❷ speed 2.
2. Prepare a bechamel sauce : melt butter in a
saucepan and add the flour. Mix and add milk
when the mixture comes away a little. Cook for
8 to 10 mins stirring until the sauce thickens.
Season with salt, pepper and nutmeg, add the
cheese and mix. Remove from heat and add the
egg yolks one by one.
3. Fit the whisk attachment (or the whipping
disk) to the processor. Pour the egg whites and
a pinch of salt into the bowl. Select speed 5 /
❷ speed 2 and beat until the egg whites are
stiff. Gently fold in the stiff egg whites to the
previous mixture. Pour into the soufflé dish and
bake for 35 to 40 mins. Serve straight away.

Onion tart

SERVES 6

Pastry
200g flour, 100g butter
Salt, 50ml water
Filling
250g onions
20g butter, 3 eggs
150g fresh cream, 150g milk
2 sprigs parsley,
Salt and pepper

PREPARATION : 20 mins
COOKING TIME : 40 mins

1. Make the pastry (see page 13) and leave to
rest.
2. Preheat the oven at 210°C (Gas Mark 7. Peel
the onions, stand them upright in the feeder
tube and slice them using the thick slicing
blade at speed 4 / ❷ speed 1. Dip them in
boiling water for 5 mins then drain them. Rince
them under cold water and drain them again.
3. Roll out the pastry into a greased flan dish of
25cm diameter. Prick the base and edges with a
fork and bake the pastry for 15 mn. Then turn
down the oven to 180°C (Gas mark 6).
4. While the pastry's baking, melt the butter in
a saucepan and cook the onions for 10 mins
stirring continuously. Chop the parsley in the
mini-chopper in short bursts at speed 4.
5. Fit the whisk attachment (or the whipping
disk) to the processor, beat the eggs for 10 secs
on speed 4 / ❷ speed 1, then add cream, milk,
parsley, salt and pepper and mix for 20 secs
Spread out the onions on the pre-cooked pastry
and pour over the cream. Put the dish into the
oven to bake for 30 to 35 mins.
Serve hot with a salad.

▷ *You can add 20g to 30g of sliced cheese
(cheddar for instance) for the filling.*

Quiche lorraine

SERVES 6

Pastry
200g flour
100g butter
1 pinch of salt, 50ml water
Filling
180g lean smoked bacon
3 eggs
150ml milk
200g fresh cream
Nutmeg, salt, peppper

PREPARATION : 15 mins
COOKING TIME : 45 mins

1. Prepare the pastry (see page 13) and leave it to stand for 30 mins. Preheat the oven at 210°C (Gas Mark 7).
2. Roll out the pastry in a Ø 25cm greased flan dish. Prick the base and pinch down the edges with a fork. Bake the pastry for 15 mins.
3. Dice the bacon and brown in a frying pan without adding any fat. Drain on a paper towel.
4. Fit the whisk attachment (or the whipping disk) to the processor and beat the eggs during 20 secs on speed 3 / ❷ speed 1. Stop the processor and add milk, cream, salt, pepper and some grated nutmeg. Beat 15 secs. Spread the diced bacon over the precooked pastry base and pour over the cream. Lower the oven temperature to 200°C and bake the quiche for 30 mins. Serve hot.

▷ *Halve the amount of bacon and add stoned prunes.*
▷ *Fill the precooked tart base with diced ham and crumbled roquefort. Salt the cream lightly.*
▷ *Replace the bacon with button mushrooms or wild mushrooms sautéed in butter.*
▷ *Mix bacon and leeks or endives cooked in butter.*

Pizza

SERVES 4 TO 6

300g bread dough
1 large can of peeled tomatoes
1 onion, 1 garlic clove
2 tablespoons olive oil
1 pinch of sugar, 1 sprig thyme
1 teaspoon of cornflour
150g mozzarella cheese
8 anchovies in oil, 16 black olives
Oregano, salt and pepper

PREPARATION : 15 mins
COOKING TIME : 30 mins
DOUGH TO STAND : 15 mins

1. Prepare the dough as indicated on page 12. You will require 300 g. Leave it to stand for 15 mins then knead it quickly and roll it out into a circle 28 cm in diameter on a baking sheet.
2. Fit the processor with the metal blade. Drain and seed the tomatoes, put them into the bowl and chop them coarsely using the *Pulse* button 4 to 5 times on speed 4.
3. Peel and chop the onion and the clove of garlic. Heat up 1 tablespoon of oil in a frying pan and gently fry the onion and garlic for 1 min then add tomatoes, cornflour, sugar, thyme, salt and pepper. Cook over medium heat until you get a fairly thick pulp.
4. Cut the mozzarella in thin slices. Preheat the oven at 240°C (Gas Mark 8). Brush the dough surface with oil. Spread the tomato pulp over the dough. Garnish with thin strips of cheese and anchovies (in star), sprinkle with oregano and olives. Pour 1 tablespoon of olive oil on top and bake for 15 to 20 mins.

▷ *You can vary the recipe in a variety of ways by garnishing with saucisson, peperoni or chorizo, ham, seafood, artichokes and mushrooms in oil, peppers, onions, capers...*

FISH, SHELLFISH

Shrimp mousse

SERVES 4

200g pink shelled shrimps
(fresh or frozen)
3 sprigs of parsley
100g fresh cream
2 egg whites
1 teaspoon oil
Chervil and lemon to decorate
Salt, pepper

PREPARATION : 10 mins
COOKING TIME : 30 mins

1. Thaw the shrimps if necessary. Drain and wipe them. Wash, dry and break off the parsley. Put aside 8 whole shrimps. Fit the metal blade to the processor and place the other shrimps into the bowl. Add the parsley, salt and pepper. Set on speed 5 / ❷ speed 2, and mix during 30 secs to obtain a purée. Stop the mixing several times to gather the mixture into the centre.
2. Add the cream and mix using 3 to 4 short bursts of the *Pulse*. Season to taste and pour the mixture into a salad bowl. Preheat the oven at 150°C (Gas mark 5).
3. Fit the whisk attachment (or the whipping disk) on the processor and pour the egg whites into the bowl. Add a pinch of salt, select speed 5/ ❷ speed 2 and beat the egg whites to a stiff snow, then carefully add to the shrimp cream.
4. Lightly oil 4 ramekins (Ø 9 cm). Put 2 shrimps in each ramekin and cover with the shrimp mousse. Place the ramekins on a simmering bain-marie and cook in the oven for 30 mins. Leave to cool.
5. Decorate with a few sprigs of chervil and very thin slices of lemon. Serve the mousse on its own or accompanied with cucumber purée or tomato purée (flesh mixed with seasoning and chervil).

Saint-Jacques and leek cream

SERVES 4

3 leeks
1 pinch curry
150ml milk
1 tablespoon single cream
1 teaspoon olive oil
12 good sized scallop shells
1 tablespoon snipped chervil
Salt and pepper

PREPARATION : 10 mins
COOKING TIME : 15 mins

1. Ask the fishmonger to open the scallop shells for you. Quickly wash the scallops and dry them on kitchen paper.
2. Peel the leeks keeping only the white and soft green parts. You will require 120g. Fit the processor with the thick slicing blade. Place the leeks vertically in the feeder tube and slice them on speed 4 / ❷ speed 2.
3. Put the chopped leeks into a saucepan with the milk, salt and pepper. Cook for 10 to 12 mins until the leeks are soft. Pour them into the mixing bowl, add the cream and the curry. Set on speed 5 / ❷ speed 2 and mix for 20 secs.
4. Pour the mixture into a small saucepan and reheat over a low heat while the scallops are cooking.
5. Heat the oil in a pan and cook the scallops until the flesh becomes opaque. Season with salt and pepper. Surround the scallops with the leeks mixture and sprinkle with the snipped chervil. Serve straight away.

Cod with tomatoes

SERVES 4

600g fresh tomatoes
2 shallots
2 tablespoons olive oil
4 slices of cod (160g each)
1 tablespoon lemon juice
1 bayleaf, 1 sprig thyme
1 tablespoon chopped parsley
Salt, pepper

PREPARATION : 10 mins
COOKING TIME: 10 mins

1. Boil and peel the tomatoes then seed and quarter them. Fit the metal knife on the processor. Peel the shallots and put them into the bowl. Select speed 5 / ❷ speed 2, chop the shallots and take them out. Coarsely chop the tomatoes using the *Pulse* button.
2. Heat 1 tablespoon of oil in a frying pan and cook the shallots over a low heat for 2 mins. Add the tomatoes, mix and season with salt and pepper.
3. Season the fish pieces and place them on the tomatoes. Add the crumbled bayleaf and the finely cut thyme. Sprinkle with a tablespoon of oil. Cover and cook for 8 to 10 mins on a low heat.
4. To serve lay the fish on top of the softened tomato mixture and sprinkle with parsley. Serve with fried courgettes, steamed potatoes or rice.

▷ *You can add a little chopped pimento, stoned black olives or capers to the tomato sauce...*

Stuffed trout

SERVES 2

2 cleaned trouts·480g
10g decrusted bread
1 celery stick 30g
30g mushrooms
2 sprigs parsley
(or parsley and tarragon)
1 tablespoon of oil
1 knob butter to grease the dish
2 tablespoons of dry white wine
Salt and pepper

PREPARATION : 10 mins
COOKING TIME : 20 mins

1. Prepare the stuffing mixture : peel and cut the celery into pieces. Clean the mushrooms. Fit the metal blade to the processor then peel the shallot and put it into the bowl. Add the bread, parsley, the mushrooms and the celery. Select speed 5 / ❷ speed 2 and chop the vegetables using the *Pulse* button.
2. Preheat the oven at 210°C (Gas Mark 7). Heat the oil in a saucepan and cook the vegetables covered for 5 mins. Season with salt and pepper.
3. Leave to cool and stuff the trout. Place the stuffed fish in a greased oven dish. Pour the white wine over the fish and bake in the oven for 15 mins. Serve the stuffed trout with steamed potatoes and fine herbs.

Smoked fish pie

SERVES 4

600g smoked haddock
800g potatoes
50g butter
450ml milk
1 tablespoon capers
2 nice sprigs parsley
2 tablespoons fresh cream
2 tablespoons lemon juice
Nutmeg
Salt and pepper

PREPARATION : 15 mins
COOKING TIME : 45 mins
Allow half a day before.

1. Leave the haddock to soak in cold water for a half day to remove the salt. Change the water from time to time.
2. Peel and cut the potatoes into cubes and cook them in boiling salted water for 25 mins, then fit the maxipress with the tray and the large hole extractor disk. Set on speed 1 and put the potatoes in the feeder tube. Mash the potatoes to a purée by adding 50ml of milk and some of the water used to boil the potatoes, in order to obtain the desired consistency. Season to taste and add the grated nutmeg and 30g butter cut into pieces. Mix.
3. While the potatoes are cooking drain the fish. Put the fish into a saucepan with 400ml of milk. You can eventually add some water in order to cover the fish. Cook for 12 to 15 mins.
4. Preheat the oven at 210°C (Gas Mark 7). When the fish is cooked strain it, remove the skin and take off the flesh. Wash, wipe and break off the parsley, and chop, in short bursts, in the mini-chopper, on speed 3.
5. Put the fish in a salad bowl and add the cream, parsley, capers and the lemon juice. Carefully mix and lay the filling in an oven dish (21cm x 16 cm). Cover with the purée mixture and place knobs of butter on top of the purée. Serve with lettuce.

Salmon with mushrooms

SERVES 4

350g button mushrooms
1/2 lemon
15g butter
100g fresh cream
4 slabs of salmon 130g each taken from a thick fillet
1 tablespoon olive oil
Chervil
Salt and pepper

PREPARATION : 10 mins
COOKING TIME : 10 mins

1. Clean the mushrooms. Fit the thick slicing blade on the processor and slice the mushrooms on speed 4 / ❷ speed 1. Sprinkle them with lemon juice to avoid discolouring.
2. Melt the butter in a frying pan and add the mushrooms and their juice. Cook over a medium heat for 5 to 6 mins. They must stay a little firm. Add the cream, season with salt and pepper and heat for 2 mins.
3. During this time heat the olive oil in a pan and when it is very hot cook the slabs of salmon. Season to taste.
4. Lay the mushrooms on the plates, then place the slabs of salmon on top. Garnish with chervil.

Fish in papillotes

SERVES 4

carrots (200g)
2 small courgettes (200g)
1 lemon
30g butter
12 coriander seeds
4 white fish fillets (110g each)
Salt and pepper

PREPARATION : 10 mins
COOKING TIME : 15 mins

1. Cut 4 sheets of greaseproof paper large
enough to enclose the fillets and vegetables.
Preheat the oven at 230°C (Gas Mark 7/8).
2. Fit the coarse grating disk in the processor
Peel the carrots. Wash the courgettes but do not
peel. Cut the vegetables in long pieces 6 to 7 cm
long and lay them flat in the lid feeder tube.
Grate the carrots at speed 4 and the courgettes
at speed 5 / ❷ speed 2.
3. Arrange a little julienne of vegetables on each
sheet of paper, lay the fish fillet on top and
cover with vegetables. Season with salt and
pepper and sprinkle with the lightly crushed
coriander seeds. Add a knob of butter on top
and sprinkle a little lemon juice. Wrap the
fillets and vegetables in their papillotes. Put
them in an oven dish and bake for 15 mins in
the oven. Serve in papillotes.

▷ *You may prepare this recipe using cod fillets,
salmon, coalfish, etc... Change cooking time to
suit.*

Fish in papillotes

MEAT, POULTRY

Pork chops with sage

SERVES 4

4 fillet pork chops
10 fresh sage leaves
5 rusks (45g), 1 small egg
1 medium onion (40g)
3 teaspoons oil, 1 knob butter
Salt and pepper

PREPARATION : 10 mins
COOKING TIME : 12 mins

1. Fit the metal blade on the processor. Put the sage leaves, rusks, salt and pepper in the mixing bowl. Select speed 5 / ❷ speed 2 and chop for 15 secs twice. Lay the mixture on a plate.
2. Break the egg into a plate and beat. Coat the pork chops in the egg first and then in the sage mixture. Coat well.
3. Heat 3 teaspoons of oil in a pan. When it is hot add the chops and brown briskly on both sides then lower the heat and cook slowly for 5 or 6 mins each side.
4. During this time peel the onion. Fit the thick slicing blade on the processor. Put the onion whole into the feeder tube, set the speed at 4 / ❷ speed 2 and press with the pusher. Take the onion rings off.
5. Heat a knob of butter in another pan and fry the onion rings. Drain the onion rings on kitchen paper. Serve with potato galettes (page 46) or unsweetened apple purée.

ROST PORK WITH SAGE : cook a rost pork fillet with onions, 600g potatoes in thick slices and 15 snipped sage leaves.

Quick chili con carne

SERVES 6

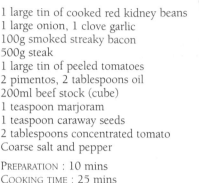

1 large tin of cooked red kidney beans
1 large onion, 1 clove garlic
100g smoked streaky bacon
500g steak
1 large tin of peeled tomatoes
2 pimentos, 2 tablespoons oil
200ml beef stock (cube)
1 teaspoon marjoram
1 teaspoon caraway seeds
2 tablespoons concentrated tomato
Coarse salt and pepper

PREPARATION : 10 mins
COOKING TIME : 25 mins

1. Peel the onion, garlic and pimentos. Cut the steak and the bacon into pieces. Fit the metal blade in the processor and chop the meat for 10 to 15 secs at speed 5 / ❷ speed 2, then give 4 to 5 short bursts using the *Pulse* button. Take the meat out and chop the onion and the garlic. Then chop the pimentos on their own. Put aside.
2. Put the drained peeled tomatoes (keep the juice) into the bowl and chop coarsely using the *Pulse* button. Prepare the stock.
3. Heat the oil in a stewpan and slighly cook the onion, garlic, bacon and chopped meat for 3 to 4 mins. Then add the pimentos, tomatoes, marjoram, caraway, salt and pepper. Leave to cook a few minutes then pour the tomato juice and the stock in which you have diluted the concentrated tomato. Cook for 15 mins.
4. Then add the kidney beans (rinsed and drained) and mix. Leave to cook a further 10 mins stirring 2 or 3 times. Serve very hot.

▷ *You can replace the fresh pimentos with dried chopped pimentos or 3 tablespoons of chilli sauce.*

Hamburgers with mustard

SERVES 4

1 shallot
4 sprigs parsley
650g steak
2 tablespoons white mustard
1 egg
1 tablespoon flour
Salt and pepper

PREPARATION : 10 mins
COOKING TIME : 5 mins

1. Fit the metal blade on the processor. Peel the shallots; wash and dry the parsley. Put them in the bowl and chop at speed 5 / ❷ speed 2. Cut the meat into pieces and chop at the same speed for 10 to 15 secs.
2. Add the mustard, egg, salt and pepper. Mix them using the Pulse button. Shape 4 hamburgers and flour them lighly. Cook them in a mixture of butter and oil.

AMERICAN STYLE: cook a steak hamburger in a pan. Heat a hamburger bun or roll in the oven for 5 mins. Then smear the 2 pieces with mayonnaise. Place on the lower part of the bun in the following order : chopped lettuce, cheese, sliced soft gherkin, chopped onion, ketchup, steak, cheese, gherkins and tomato slices. Close the bun and put in the oven for 2 mins.

MOROCCAN STYLE: mix together 700g of minced meat (beef or lamb) and 1 small onion, 1 clove of garlic, 20 leaves of fresh coriander, 8 leaves of mint (chopped); pinch of chili pepper, 1 teaspoon crushed cumin, salt, pepper and 1 egg. Make meatballs out of the mixture and put on a skewer for grilled or barbecued kebabs.

Chopping

1. Cut the food to be minced into pieces: up to 600g meat (with sinews removed), raw or cooked fish, vegetables, cheese...Select speed 5 / ❷ speed 2. For the best chopping results use the Pulse button in short bursts.

2. Chop 10 to 30 secs. The longer you chop, the finer the mixture. For a coarse mixture set the speed to 5 and use short bursts of the Pulse button.

Osso bucco

SERVES 4

4 slices of calf shin (1 kg 400)
3 tablespoons of olive oil
2 onions
2 celery sticks
300g carrots
500g fresh tomatoes
2 garlic cloves
100ml dry white wine
200ml of beef stock
1 bouquet garni (parsley, thyme, bayleaf)
1/2 lemon peel
1/2 orange peel
3 sprigs of parsley
Salt and pepper

PREPARATION : 15 mins
COOKING TIME : 1 H 30 mins

1. Heat the oil in a saucepan and brown the slices of calf shin on either side.
2. Peel the onions, celery and carrots. Cut the onions in two. Fit the metal blade on the processor and coarsely chop the vegetables on speed 5 / ❷ speed 2.
3. When the meat is brown put it aside and pour the vegetables in the saucepan. Cover and simmer for 5 mins. Peel, seed the tomatoes and put them in the processor bowl with the metal blade. Select speed 5 / ❷ speed 2 and crush the tomatoes in 5 to 6 short bursts using the *Pulse* button. Add them to the saucepan with 1 chopped garlic clove. Put the meat back into the saucepan, season with salt and pepper. Mix and pour in the wine and the hot stock. Add the bouquet garni, cover and leave to simmer for 1 hour 30 mins.
4. Put the fruit peel, 1 clove garlic and the washed and dried parsley into the mini-chopper. Chop finely on speed 3.
5. Serve the meat onto a dish (remove the bouquet garni) and sprinkle with the peel and parsley mixture. Serve hot with rice or pasta.

Rolled veal

SERVES 6

1 large thick veal escalope (600g)
10 rashers of smoked streaky bacon (100g)
2 carrots (peeled 240g)
180g of celery sticks (peeled 140g)
2 sprigs fresh thyme
10g butter, 1 tablespoon oil
1 bouquet garni, 1 onion
150ml beef stock
Salt and pepper

PREPARATION : 20 mins
COOKING TIME : 30 mins

1. Ask your butcher to cut a large thick escalope and to cut it through its width in order to obtain a large rectangle 1/2cm thick (about 22 cm x 26 cm).
2. Peel the carrots and cut them in sticks. Peel the celery sticks with the potato peeler and cut them in the same way. Fit the metal blade on the processor, put the vegetables in the mixing bowl, set the speed on 5 / ❷ speed 2 and chop them coarsely.
3. Cover the escalope with bacon rashers then the vegetables on top. Season with salt and pepper and sprinkle with thyme leaves. Then roll the escalope lengthwise and tie the obtained roast with fine string.
4. Heat butter and oil in a saucepan, cook the roast all golden all over, then add the chopped onion and any remaining chopped vegetables, beef stock and bouquet garni. Cover and cook for 30 to 35 mins. The roll can be eaten hot or cold.

▷ *You can put the cooking stock through the blender and add some fresh cream to make a sauce.*

Chicken pie

SERVES 4 TO 6

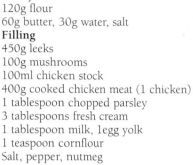

Pastry
120g flour
60g butter, 30g water, salt
Filling
450g leeks
100g mushrooms
100ml chicken stock
400g cooked chicken meat (1 chicken)
1 tablespoon chopped parsley
3 tablespoons fresh cream
1 tablespoon milk, 1egg yolk
1 teaspoon cornflour
Salt, pepper, nutmeg

PREPARATION : 20 mins
COOKING TIME : 30 mins

1. Prepare the pastry as indicated on page 13.
Leave to stand in a cool place for 1 hour.
2. Peel the leeks and keep the white and soft
green part only (you will have 200g). Cut in
slices with the thick slicing blade on speed 4 /
❷ speed 1. Clean the mushrooms and slice
them in the same way.
3. Put the leeks and the mushrooms into a
small saucepan, add the hot chicken stock,
cover and cook for 8 to 10 mins.
4. Preheat the oven at 220°C (Gas Mark 7/8).
Cut the cooked chicken into pieces of 1 to
2 cm. Spread the pastry out to make a circle of
Ø 21cm , keep the excess for decoration. Add
the chicken to the vegetables with the parsley,
cream, salt, pepper and some grated nutmeg.
Stir the cornflour into the milk and add to the
mixture. Mix and pour into a pie dish Ø 19 cm,
depth 4cm. Brush the sides of the dish with egg
yolk mixed with 2 tablespoons of water.
5. Place the pastry on the dish and press the sides
to stick on the walls of the dish. Use excess pastry
for decorating and brush with the diluted egg. Put
the dish in the oven and cook for 25 mins.

Stuffed chicken

SERVES 4

1 chicken (1 kg 400) with liver
150g button mushrooms
100g cooked ham
50g raw ham
3 sprigs parsley
20g decrusted bread
10g butter
Salt and pepper

PREPARATION : 10 mins
COOKING TIME : 50 mins

1. Clean and wash the mushrooms. Cut the raw
and cooked ham into pieces. Wash and dry the
parsley and remove the leaves. Fit the metal
blade on the processor and chop the liver, ham,
parsley, mushrooms and bread for 10 secs at
speed 5 / ❷ speed 2.
2. Preheat the oven at 220°C (Gas Mark 7).
Melt the butter in a frying pan and fry the
stuffing for 5 mins on a medium heat. Season
with salt and pepper and leave to cool.
3. Once the stuffing has cooled, stuff the
chicken and sew it up (or plug with a ball of
greaseproof paper). Place the chicken in an
oven dish and cook it in the oven for 45 to
50 mins.

▷ *You can also roast sliced potatoes in the oven
dish with the chicken.*

▷ *To gain time stuff 4 chicken escalopes (laid
flat) with the same stuffing and cook in a frying
pan for 15 to 20 mins.*

Chicken curry

SERVES 6

1 chicken cut into pieces
(1 kg 100), 1 large onion
1 garlic clove, 2 tomatoes
2 tablespoons oil
2 teaspoons Madras curry powder
1 pinch cayenne pepper
1 sprig thyme
1 yoghurt
200ml chicken stock
1 apple
Salt and pepper

PREPARATION : 10 mins
COOKING TIME : 30 mins

1. Heat the oil in a saucepan and fry the
chicken pieces until golden. Peel the onion and
clove garlic. Skin and seed the tomatoes.
Prepare the spices and heat up the stock.
2. Fit the metal blade on the processor , chop
the onion and garlic at speed 5 / 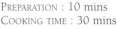 speed 2 for
20 secs. Put aside. Chop the tomatoes coarsely
using 5 to 6 bursts of the *Pulse* button.
3. Remove the chicken from the saucepan and
put the onion and the garlic in. Fry for 2 mins
stirring all the time and add spices. Leave to
cook a further minute, continue stirring and
add the tomatoes, thyme, yoghurt and the hot
chicken stock. Return the chicken to the
saucepan. Stir, cover and cook on a medium
heat for 20 mins.
4. Peel and quarter the apple. Stand quarters
upright in the feeder tube and slice using the
thick slicing blade on speed 4 / 2 peed 1.
After the chicken has cooked for 20 mins add
the apple and leave to simmer for 10 mins.
Serve the curry very hot with rice, coconut and
chutneys.

Chicken curry

▷ *You can also add other spices : 6 cardamom
seeds, 1/2 teaspoon of caraway seeds, 1 teaspoon
of fresh grated ginger, 2 cloves…*

▷ *Replace half of the apple with half of a
banana*

▷ *To gain time make the same mixture with
4 chicken escalopes cut into pieces (in the Chinese
way), reduce the chicken stock to 50ml. Cook for
5 mins, add the apple and put back for 10 mins*

Making purée

1. Fit the maxipress large hole disk and place the tray on the lid feeder tube. Start the processor on speed 1 and gradually put in the cut and cooked food.

2. Pour in a little of the cooking water to rectify the purée consistency. You can prepare up to 1 kg cooked vegetables (or 500g soft fleshed fruit).

3. Fit the metal blade and select speed 3 / ❷ speed 1. Pour the cooked vegetables into the bowl and start the processor. Gradually increase the speed to 5 / ❷ speed 2. You can make carrot, celery and pea purée... For potatoes containing starch, it is better to use the maxipress.

VEGETABLES

Mashed potatoes with milk

SERVES 4

800g potatoes
300ml milk,
1 teaspoon coarse salt
40g butter
Pepper

PREPARATION : 10 mins
COOKING TIME : 25 mins

1. Peel the potatoes, cut them into pieces and wash them. Then put them in a saucepan. Cover with cold water and sprinkle with coarse salt. Bring to the boil, skimming off the froth at the beginning of cooking. Leave to cook for 10 mins.
2. Heat the milk on a low heat. After 10 mins drain the potatoes which are still firm. Return them to the saucepan and pour in the warm milk. Cook for 15 mins until the potatoes are soft.
3. Fit the maxipress with the large hole disk. Select speed 1. Start the processor. Add the potatoes gradually. When this is almost finished pour in the milk used to cook the potatoes, to obtain the desired consistency.
4. Add pepper, check the salt seasoning. If it is not sufficiently salty add some salt which has been mixed with warm milk. Next fold in pieces of butter. Serve straight away.

SPINACH PURÉE : prepare 1 kg of spinach, peel 200g of potatoes and cook them in salty boiling water. Drain thoroughly. Fit the maxipress large hole disk or the metal blade on the processor and work the mixture until you obtain a purée. Add 2 tablespoons of fresh cream.

Carrot purée

SERVES 4

750g carrots, 100g fresh cream
Salt and pepper

PREPARATION : 10 mins
COOKING TIME : 25 mins

1. Peel and cut the carrots into pieces and cook in boiling, salted water for 20 to 25 mins.
2. Drain the carrots and put them in the mixing bowl fitted with the metal blade.
Select speed 5 / ❷ speed 2 and blend adding some of the cooking water as required. Season with salt and pepper and fold in the cream. You may also use the maxipress.

▷ *Add 3 tablespoons of chopped parsley*
▷ *You can also mix together carrots and tomatoes, carrots and pumpkin or carrots and potatoes.*
▷ *Flavour the purée with a pinch of paprika, caraway seeds or curry.*

Pasta with vegetables

SERVES 4

1 good-sized leek 240g
1 small courgette 140g, 2 carrots 200g
200g spaghetti or tagliatelle
1 tablespoon olive oil, 20g butter
Salt and pepper

PREPARATION : 10 mins
COOKING TIME : 10 mins

1. Fit the thick slicing blade on the processor. Peel and wash the vegetables : do not peel the courgettes; keep only the white and soft green part of the leek, i.e. 120g. Cut the carrots and leeks into sticks of 7 cm and place them flat in the feeder tube. Adjust the speed to 4 / ❷ speed 2 and cut into slices. Cook for 2 mins in

Making purée

1. The mini-chopper allows you to prepare up to 100g purée for baby food. Pour the cooked vegetables into the chopper and gradually add the meat, ham or fish.

2. Select speed 2 to 5 or use the Pulse button for best results.

salted boiling water. Drain them and put them under cold water. Drain them again.
2. Place the courgettes upright into the feeder tube and cut into round slices. Heat the oil in a pan and fry the courgettes for 8 mins.
3. Cook the pasta in salted boiling water. Drain the pasta and put it in a salad bowl containing 20g butter and mix. Add the vegetables and carefully mix in. Season to taste. This mixture goes with meat as well as with fish.
▷ *You can make the same recipes with peppers that you shall cut in slices (thick slicing blade).*

Broccoli gateau

SERVES 6

600 g broccoli
2 small white onions
60g gruyère cheese
2 sprigs parsley
200ml milk, 3 eggs
Nutmeg
Salt and pepper

PREPARATION : 15 mins
COOKING TIME : 40 mins

1. Strip off outer leaves and wash the broccoli, then divide the head into florets and cut the stalks into cubes. Wash and dry the parsley and take the leaves off. Peel the onions and cut in two. Grate the cheese using the fine grating disk on speed 4 / ❷ speed 2.
2. Preheat the oven at 210°C (Gas Mark 7). Put the broccoli and the onions into a saucepan of boiling water and cook for 5 mins. Then drain the florets of broccoli with a skimming ladle and put them in an oven dish Ø 23 cm with high sides (5.5 cm). Continue to cook the stalks and the onions for another 6 mins.
3. Then drain them carefully. Place them with the parsley leaves into the processor bowl fitted with the metal blade and set the speed on 5 / ❷ speed 2. Chop for 15 secs ; stop once or twice to bring the ingredients into the centre. Then add the egg with the milk, season with salt, pepper and the grated nutmeg. Fold in the grated cheese and mix in short bursts using the *Pulse* button on speed 2.
4. Pour the mixture over the broccoli and put the mould into the oven to cook for 30 mins. This recipe can be dish on its own.

▷ *You can replace the broccoli with cauliflower (allow a longer cooking time).*

Courgettes au gratin with spices

SERVES 4

600g courgettes
20g butter
150g single cream
2 eggs
1 sprig thyme
2 pinches of curry
2 pinches of powdered caraway
2 pinches of grated nutmeg
Salt and pepper

PREPARATION : 10 mins
COOKING TIME : 15 mins

1. Wash and dry the courgettes and cut off the tips. Fit the thin slicing blade and set on speed 4 / ❷ speed 2. Stand the courgettes upright in the feeder tube and cut thin slices.
2. Melt the butter in a saucepan. Fry the courgettes and stir. Sprinkle with caraway, nutmeg and curry. Mix and cook for 8 to 10 mins, stirring from time to time. Remove from heat and arrange the courgettes in a greased oven dish (16 x 21 cm).
Sprinkle with thyme.
3. Switch the oven grill on. Whip the cream with eggs, salt and pepper in the bowl fitted with the whisk attachment (or the whipping disk) during 20 secs on speed 2 / ❷ speed 1. Pour the mixture onto the courgettes. Place the dish in the oven and grill for 5 mins. This dish can be served hot or cold.

Potatoes au gratin

SERVES 5

800g potatoes
200ml milk
1 small garlic clove
125g fresh cream
2 egg yolks
Grated nutmeg
30g emmenthal or cheddar cheese
15g butter
Salt and pepper

PREPARATION : 10 mins
COOKING TIME : 50 mins

1. Fit the fine grating blade to the processor, select speed 4 / ❷ speed 2 and grate the cheese. Keep aside.
2. Replace the grater with the thick slicing disk. Peel and wash the potatoes. Stand them upright in the feeder tube and slice them on speed 4 / ❷ speed 2. Preheat the oven at 210°C (Gas-Mark 7).
3. Cut the garlic clove in half and use it to rub an oven dish (16 cm x 21 cm). Then cut the rest into thin slices. Arrange the potatoes in the oven dish with the garlic slices.
4. Pour the cream, milk, egg yolks, salt, pepper and grated nutmeg into the bowl fitted with the whisk attachment (or the whipping disk). Select speed 2 / ❷ speed 1 and whisk for 15 secs. Pour the mixture onto the potatoes. Sprinkle the dish with grated cheese and a few butter knobs. Cook for 50 mins.

▷ *You may also cut the potatoes with the thin slicing disk on speed 4 / ❷ speed 1.*

▷ *You can cook the dish in a microwave oven at 620 Watts + grill for 22 mins on microwave + grill mode.*

▷ *Halve the quantity of potatoes with leeks or celeriac.*

Potatoes au gratin

Potato Galette

SERVES 4 TO 6

800g potatoes
1 small onion (40g)
20g butter
1 teaspoon oil
Salt and pepper

PREPARATION : 5 mins
COOKING TIME : 20 mins

1. Peel and halve the onion. Peel and wash the potatoes. Fit the coarse grating disk on the processor. Place the potatoes and the onion vertically into the feeder tube and grate on speed 4 / ❷ speed 1.
2. Melt the butter and oil in a pan Ø 24 cm. Add the potatoes and the onion, spread out and compress to form a pancake. Season with salt, pepper and cook the first side for 8 mins. Turn the galette by sliding it onto a plate and cook the other side for 8 to 10 mins. Slip the rest of the butter in little knobs between the pan and the galette circumference. It will melt and run underneath the galette. Season with salt and pepper.

POTATO GALETTES WITH SMOKED BACON : grate the potatoes with the fine grater. Mix them with 100g chopped bacon and 50g chopped onion. Add 2 eggs, salt and pepper. Make small piles of potatoes in the pan with the help of 2 tablespoons. Flatten them and cook until golden on both sides. Repeat several times.

Cabbage with bacon and juniper

SERVES 4

 small green cabbage 800g
(net 600g)
1 carrot
100g lean smoked bacon
8 juniper berries (optional)
20g butter
Salt and pepper

PREPARATION : 10 mins
COOKING TIME : 40 mins

1. Remove the outer leaves and quarter the cabbage. Take out the hard central part. Wash the cabbage pieces. Drain well and place them upright in the feeder tube. Cut the cabbage in thin strips using the thick slicing blade on speed 4 / ❷ speed 1. Peel the carrot and slice it.
2. Put the cabbage and the carrot slices into a large saucepan of boiling water and leave them for 6 to 7 mins. Drain them, run under cold water and drain again.
3. Finely dice the bacon. Heat a frying pan and brown the bacon for 3 mins. Add the cabbage, carrot, butter knobs, 150 ml water and the juniper berries. Season with salt and pepper, mix and cook on a low heat for 30 mins. Serve with roast pork or smoked pork shoulder, sausages or codfish steaks.

DESSERTS

Floating islands

SERVES 4

1/4 litre milk, 1/2 vanilla pod, 3 eggs
50g caster sugar, 10g icing sugar
Caramel
100g sugar cubes

PREPARATION : 10 mins
COOKING TIME : 10 mins

1. Pour the milk into a saucepan with the half
vanilla pod and bring to the boil. In the bowl
fitted with the whisk attachment (or the
whipping disk) beat the egg yolks with the
caster sugar at speed 3 / ❷ speed 1 until the
mixture whitens. Pour the warm milk onto the
egg yolks and switch on at speed 1.
2. Pour the mixture into a saucepan and cook
over a low heat for approximately 8 mins until
the cream coats the spoon. It must not boil.
Pour the mixture immediately into the serving
dish through a sieve. Let it cool and put it in
the fridge.
3. Clean the bowl and the whisk. Pour the egg
whites, add a pinch of salt and beat to a stiff
snow at speed 5 / ❷ speed 2. Then fold in
icing sugar and beat again for a few seconds.
4. Heat some milk in a saucepan. Using a
tablespoon place little mounds of egg whites on
the simmering milk and cook them for one
minute on each side.
5. Put the moistened sugar cubes into a little
saucepan and cook them until you obtain a
brown clear caramel. Place the egg whites on
the cold custard and coat them with caramel.

▷ *You can replace the caramel with a red fruit
sauce or pomegranate seeds.*

Whisking

1. Egg whites : pour the egg whites (from 1 to
7) into the bowl fitted with the whisk attachment, add a pinch of salt and select speed 5.

2. Switch on and whisk until you obtain a stiff
snow (1 mins 30 to 2 mins).

3. In the same way whip the egg whites with
the whipping disk at speed 5 / ❷ speed 2.

Making a fruit coulis

1. Fit the maxipress with the small size hole extractor disk. Place the tray on the feeder tube and start the processor on speed 1. Gradually add the fruit.

2. You can prepare up to 500g strawberries, raspberries, cherries, redcurrants and other berries...Use the medium size hole extractor disk to make a pineapple coulis.

3. With the blender attachment : pour the fruit, sugar, a little water and lemon juice. Start to blend at speed 1 and gradually increase the speed to 5 / ❷ speed 2. Depending on the fruit and the desired consistency sieve the coulis.

Fresh raspberry coulis

FOR 300G COULIS

250g raspberries
20 to 30g caster sugar (depending on taste)
1teaspoon lemon juice

PREPARATION : 5 mins

1. Quickly wash the raspberries. Drain and put into a salad bowl with the sugar and lemon. Mix well.
2. Fit the maxipress with the small hole extractor disk and start at speed 1. Gradually add the contents of the salad bowl. A little mineral water may be added depending on the required consistency.

▷ *Do the same to make strawberry coulis. For a redcurrant or blackcurrant purée you will get a better result if you burst the berries first by heating, before reducing them into a purée.*

Red fruit soup

SERVES 4

250g raspberries
300g strawberries
150g redcurrants
40 to 50g caster sugar
1 pinch of powdered cinnamon
1 tablespoon lemon juice

PREPARATION : 10 mins

1. Prepare a coulis with 200g raspberries, 50g stalked redcurrants, the caster sugar blended with the cinnamon, the lemon juice and 100ml mineral water. Proceed as indicated above.
2. Wash and stalk the strawberries, halve or quarter them upright depending on their size. Quickly wash the rest of the raspberries and

redcurrants and put all the fruit into a salad
bowl. Add the coulis and mix carefully.
Refrigerate before serving.
Decorate with fresh mint.

Stewed apple compote

SERVES 6

800g apples of different varieties
(Cox, Canada, Boskoop)
1 tablespoon lemon juice
1 pinch powdered cinnamon (optional)

PREPARATION : 10 mins
COOKING TIME : 15 mins

1. Peel the apples, cut them into pieces and put
them in a saucepan. Add the cinnamon, lemon
juice, 100ml water and put on heat. Cover and
cook until the apples are soft (approximately
15 mins or 7 mins in a microwave at 900 Watts).
2. Leave to cool a little, then pour them into the
processor bowl fitted with the metal blade. Set
the speed on 5 / ❷ speed 2 and reduce the
fruit into a compote. The longer you mix the
fruit the finer the compote will be. If you prefer
a compote with little pieces of fruit throughout,
use the *Pulse* button. You can also use the
maxipress with the large size hole extractor disk.

SPICED APPLE COMPOTE : while cooking add
1 clove, 1 vanilla pod, a pinch of aniseed and
1 pinch of powdered ginger.

▷ *You can combine apples and pears or apples*
and dried apricots (previously soaked in water).

▷ *Put a little yoghurt or fresh cream cheese in*
small dishes, top with apple compote and
decorate with raspberries. Sprinkle over with
a few grilled almonds.

Making fruit compote

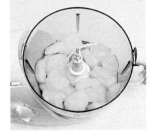

1. Use the metal blade to make fruit compote :
pour the strained cooked fruit into the bowl

2. Select speed 5 / ❷ speed 2 and blend until
you get the required finess consistency

Whipping

1. Whipped cream : pour the very cold cream into the processor bowl (put it into the freezer for a few minutes beforehand). Set the speed on 2 / ❷ speed 1 and start the processor.

2. Progressively increase the speed to 4 / ❷ speed 2. Stop when the cream forms waves (whipping time depends on the quantity).

3. In the same way whip the cream with the whipping disk.

Peach mousse

SERVES 4

7 good-sized ripe peaches
2 tablespoons lemon juice
150g very cold single cream
50g sugar
Fresh mint

PREPARATION : 15 mins

1. Peel 6 peaches, stone them and pour the fruit flesh into the processor bowl fitted with the metal blade. Sprinkle them with lemon juice. Select speed 5 / ❷ speed 2 and reduce the peaches into a purée. Add the sugar and blend again for 10 secs. Leave to chill.
2. Wash the processor bowl and replace the metal blade with the whisk attachment (or the whipping disk). Pour in the cream, set the speed on 2 / ❷ speed 1 and beat for 30 secs then increase the speed gradually to 4 / ❷ speed 1 until the cream becomes fluffy. Fold in the 2 preparations very carefully and spoon the mousse into small dishes.
3. Cut the remaining peach into slices and sprinkle with lemon juice to avoid discolouring. Use to top the mousses and decorate with a leaf of fresh mint.

▷ *You can also use strawberries, apricots, nectarines...*

▷ *To make a bavarian, add 6 g gelatine to the peach purée.*

▷ *To peel the peaches easily, dip them before during a few seconds in boiling water*

Peaches in orange jelly

SERVES 4

4 juicy oranges
1/2 lemon
2 yellow peaches
2 tablespoons sugar
6 sheets gelatine (12g)

PREPARATION : 15 mins

1. Soak the gelatine in a bowl of cold water. Fit the citrus press on the processor, set on speed 1 and squeeze the oranges. You should obtain 350ml of juice. Squeeze the lemon half. Strain 2 teaspoons of lemon juice with orange juice.
2. Peel a peach. Open it and remove the stone. Put the peach flesh into the blender attachment with the juice and the sugar. Set on speed 5 / ❷ speed 2 and blend for 15 secs, then sieve to obtain a smooth juice.
3. Peel and open the second peach. Remove the stone. Cut each half into thin slices and sprinkle with lemon juice to avoid discolouring.
4. Drain the gelatine and put it into the bowl with 2 tablespoons of water. Melt for 30 secs in the microwave and add to the orange juice while whisking with a handwhisk.
5. Lightly grease 4 ramekins (Ø 10 cm) with a brush and place 3 peach slices on the bottom of each ramekin. Cover with the orange jelly and allow to set in the refrigerator for at least 2 hours. Turn out of ramekins and garnish with fresh mint leaves.

▷ *To remove easily, dip the moulds for a few seconds in very hot water*

Citrus pressing

1. Cut the citrus fruit in two. Place one half on the cone and start on speed 1. You can extract up to 1 litre of juice without having to empty the bowl.

Rhubarb and strawberry meringue

SERVES 3 TO 4

1 bunch rhubarb (600g stripped)
70g caster sugar
200g strawberries
2 egg whites
2 heaped tablespoons icing sugar

PREPARATION : 10 mins
COOKING TIME : 15 mins

1. Strip and wash the rhubarb then cut the stalks into sticks (about 7 mm thick and 5 cm long). Cook with the sugar and 2 tablespoons water. When the rhubarb is soft, carefully strain and leave to cool in the strainer.
2. Wash and hull the strawberries. Stand upright and cut in slices. Put the strained rhubarb into a porcelain tart dish Ø 21 cm then cover the rhubarb with the strawberry slices.
3. Switch on the oven grill. Put the egg whites into the bowl fitted with the whisk attachment (or the whipping disk), set the speed to 5 / ❷ speed 2 and beat to a stiff snow. Then add the icing sugar and continue to beat for a few seconds. Spread the meringue evenly on top of the strawberries and place under the grill until golden. Serve hot or cold.

Chocolate mousse

SERVES 4 TO 6

200g plain bitter cooking chocolate
30g butter
4 eggs
40g sugar
1 tablespoon fresh cream

PREPARATION : 10 mins
COOKING TIME : 5 mins

1. Break the chocolate into pieces and melt over a bain-marie (or in a microwave) with 2 tablespoons of water. Remove from heat, add the diced butter and stir to obtain a smooth mixture.
2. In the processor bowl fitted with the whisk attachment (or the whipping disk) pour in the egg yolks and 20g sugar. Set the speed to 3 / ❷ speed 1 and mix for 30 secs, add the cream and mix for 15 secs, then lower the speed to 2 and pour in the melted chocolate through the feeder tube. Mix 20 secs and put aside.
3. Clean the processor bowl and set the speed on 5 / ❷ speed 2. Beat the egg whites until stiff snow (add a pinch of salt). At the end pour the rest of the sugar through the feeder tube and whisk for a further 10 secs. Gently fold in the beaten egg whites with the chocolate in 3 goes and leave to chill.

▷ *To flavour the mousse add a few drops of coffee essence or grated orange peel.*

CREAM CHEESE MOUSSE : with the metal blade mix 450g of 0% soft white cheese strained the day before, with 2 teaspoons honey for 1 minute at speed 3. Then fold in 100g of whipped single cream. Serve with fresh fruit.

Chocolate mousse ▷

Strawberry terrine

SERVES 4 TO 6

3 sheets of gelatine (6 g)
100ml water
80g sugar
400g strawberries
200g fresh or frozen redcurrants
100g very cold single cream

PREPARATION : 15 mins - Plan 6 hours before

1. Leave the gelatine to soak in cold water. Pour 100ml water with the sugar into a saucepan and bring to the boil. Simmer for 5 mins then pour the redcurrant into the syrup. Leave to simmer for a minute then remove from the heat.
2. Pour the mixture into the blender attachment, blend at speed 2 first / ❷ speed 1, then increase the speed to 5 / ❷ speed 2 to obtain a purée. Strain it through a sieve. Using the maxipress (with the small size hole extractor disk at speed 1) avoids you going through this last step.
3. Mix the drained and pressed gelatine sheets in the warm purée while whisking the mixture wih a handwhisk. Leave to cool.
4. Pour the mixture into the bowl fitted with the whisk attachment (or the blender disk) and whisk the cream until light and fluffy : start on speed 2 / ❷ speed 1 and increase gradually up to 4 / ❷ speed 2. Mix the whipped cream with the redcurrant purée.
5. Pour a little amount of redcurrant purée (1 cm) into the terrine and leave to set during 5 mins in the freezer. Cover with a layer of washed strawberries. Pour over another layer of cream, cover with strawberries and finish with a layer of cream on top. Tap the terrine sides lightly so that all the ingredients are evenly spaced and the cream evenly spread. Cover with the lid and chill for 6 hours. Serve the terrine in slices with a strawberry or pineapple coulis. Decorate with mint leaves.

Redcurrant sorbet

SERVES 4

500g redcurrants
70g sugar
2 tablespoons lemon juice

PREPARATION : 15 mins
COOKING TIME : 5 mins
FREEZING TIME : 20 to 30 mins

1. Wash and stalk the redcurrants. Pour 100ml water, lemon juice and sugar into a saucepan stirring well and bring to the boil, then simmer for 5 mins.
2. Add the redcurrants and continue to cook for 30 secs then remove from the heat. Fit the maxipress with the small size hole extractor disk and set on speed 1. Start the processor and gradually add the fruit and the syrup into the feeder tube fitted with the tray. Leave to cool.
3. Pour the cold purée into an ice cream churn and freeze.

STRAWBERRY SORBET : cut 500g of strawberries into pieces and put them in the blender attachment. Add the syrup (see above, reduce the sugar to 40g) and blend on speed 1 then 5 / ❷ speed 1 then 2 to obtain a purée. Sieve and leave to set in the ice cream freezer. You may also use the maxipress to make the sorbet.

KIWI FRUIT SORBET : peel and cut the ripe kiwi fruit into pieces. Put them into the bowl fitted with the metal blade. Add 40g sugar, the juice from one orange and the juice from half a lemon. Blend at maximum speed. Also use the maxipress to make the sorbet.

Profiteroles

SERVES 8

Choux pastry (See page 14)
Filling
1/2 litre vanilla ice cream
Chocolate sauce
400g plain bitter chocolate
80g butter
100g fresh cream

PREPARATION : 20 mins
COOKING TIME : 20 mins

1. Prepare the choux pastry as indicated on page 14. Bake the choux and let them cool on a rack.
2. Prepare the sauce : melt the chocolate in a saucepan over a very low heat (or in the microwave), add butter and cream. Mix until the sauce is smooth.
3. Fill each choux with a scoop of vanilla ice cream and arrange on plates. Put on the table and pour over the hot chocolate sauce.

Chocolate ice cream

SERVES 6

1/2 litre milk
5 egg yolks
80g sugar
50g unsweetened cocoa
100g fresh cream

PREPARATION : 10 mins
COOKING TIME : 8 mins
FREEZING TIME : 30 mins

1. Heat up the milk. Put the egg yolks and the sugar in the processor bowl fitted with the whisk qttachment (or the whipping disk). Beat for 30 secs on speed 2 / ❷ speed 1. Add a little

amount of boiling milk through the feeder tube, beating all the time, then pour in the rest of the milk and blend. Return the mixture to the saucepan and stirr continuously until it thickens. Do not allow the cream to boil. Once it coats the back of the spoon it is cooked.
2. Leave to cool a while then pour the mixture into the processor bowl. Add the cocoa and whip for 30 secs on speed 3 / ❷ speed 1. Add the fresh cream and whip during 15 secs. Leave the cream to cool before pouring into the ice cream churn for freezing.

VANILLA FLAVOUR : add the inside of a vanilla pod to the egg yolks and sugar mixture. Leave out the cocoa.

Pineapple fritters

SERVES 6

1 pineapple
10g baker's yeast
100g flour
150ml light lager

PREPARATION : 15 mins
COOKING TIME : 15 mins

1. Dilute the yeast with 3 tablespoons mild water. Put the flour into the processor bowl fitted with the metal blade, add the diluted yeast and start mixing on speed 2 / ❷ speed 1. Gradually add the lager into the feeder tube increasing the speed to 4 / ❷ speed 2. Leave the mixture to stand in a cool place for 30 mins at least.
2. During this time prepare a deep frying pan. Peel the pineapple, remove the " eyes ", cut the fruit into slices and quarter each slice. Dip the pieces in the mixture and fry them for 30 secs on each side. Serve with a strawberry coulis.

PASTRIES

Apple tart

SERVES 6

350g shortcrust or shortbread pastry
(see pages 13 and 14)
Filling
850g Golden Delicious or Cox's apples
1 lemon
2 tablespoons caster sugar
1 pinch of powdered cinnamon

PREPARATION : 15 mins
COOKING TIME : 45 mins

1. Preheat the oven at 200°C (Gas Mark 6-7).
Roll out the pastry in a flan case Ø 28 cm. Prick
the base and pinch down the edges with a fork
and put in the fridge for 5 to 10 mins.
2. Quarter, peel and core the apples. Fit the
thick slicing blade on the processor and select
speed 4 / ❷ speed 1. Lay the quartered apples
flat in the feeder tube and slice. Sprinkle with
lemon juice to avoid discolouring.
3. Arrange a layer of apples (using the least
attractive slices). Sprinkle with a mixed
tablespoon of sugar and cinnamon. Arrange the
best apple slices on top to make a rose like
pattern. Sprinkle the surface with sifted caster
sugar and bake for 40 mins.
Serve warm or cold with a little fresh cream.

Apple crumble

SERVES 4 TO 6

900g Golden Delicious apples
1 pinch of powdered cinnamon (optional)
2 tablespoons lemon juice
140g flour
75g sugar
75g butter at room temperature
200g raspberries

PREPARATION : 10 mins
COOKING TIME : 45 mins

1. Peel and cube the apples and put into a
saucepan with the lemon juice, the cinnamon
and 100ml water. Cover and cook for 15 mins
(or 5 mins in the microwave at 900 Watts
without adding water).
2. Fit the metal blade to the processor, pour in the
sifted flour, sugar and diced butter. Select
speed 2 / ❷ speed 1, mix the ingredients for
10 secs and increase the speed to 3 and mix until
you obtain a grainy mixture (not a smooth pastry).
Finish in some bursts to crumb the mixture.
3. Preheat the oven at 220°C (Gas Mark 7-8),
pour off the cooking juice from the apples and
arrange the fruit in a spongecake mould Ø 22 cm
(ovenproof porcelain mould or pyrex for
example). Arrange raspberries on top, then cover
the fruit with " crumble ". Bake for 35 to 45 mins.
The crumble will form a golden crunchy crust on
the fruit.

▷ *Apple crumble can be served slightly warm or
cold with a little fresh cream.*

▷ *It is still delicious the next day.*

▷ *In winter you can replace the raspberries
with frozen red fruit.*

▷ *You can replace the raspberries with
blackberries, alternate apples and apricots... or
replace the apples with rhubarb.*

Lemon tart

SERVES 6

Pastry
200g flour
100g butter
1 pinch salt
50ml water

Filling
3 untreated lemons
100g sugar, 3 eggs
1/4 litre milk
50g fresh double cream

PREPARATION : 15 mins
COOKING TIME : 45 mins

1. Prepare the pastry as indicated on page 13 and leave to stand. Preheat the oven at 210°C (Gas Mark 7). Roll out the pastry and line a Ø 25 cm flan tin. Bake the pastry for 15 mins.
2. Wash the lemons and grate the peel over the processor bowl. Install the citrus press and squeeze the lemons (you will need 100g juice). Pour the juice into a glass.
3. Fit the whisk attachment (or the whipping disk) and beat the eggs for 20 secs with the sugar at speed 3 / ❷ speed 1. Stop the processor, add milk, cream and lemon juice and beat for 15 secs until smooth.
4. Lower the oven temperature at 180°C (Gas Mark 6). Take the pastry out of the oven and pour the lemon cream on the precooked pastry. Put back in the oven for 30 to 35 mins. Leave to cool before removing from the flan tin.

▷ *Decorate the tart with slices of candied lemon in syrup.*

▷ *Use limes instead of lemons.*

▷ *To make a lemon meringue tart beat 2 egg whites stiffly with 2 tablespoons of icing sugar. Spread the meringue mixture on top of the baked tart and brown under grill.*

Apple tart

Strawberry sandwich cake

SERVES 6 TO 8

Sponge
125g granulated sugar
1 tablespoon orange blossom water
4 eggs, 15g melted butter
50g flour, 50g cornflour
Filling
300g well drained white creamed cheese
20g caster sugar
1 tablespoon orange blossom water
500g strawberries of even size
140g redcurrant jelly
20g trimmed grilled almonds

PREPARATION : 20 mins
COOKING TIME : 30 mins

1. Preheat the oven at 180°C (Gas Mark 6).
Prepare the sponge : grease and flour a round
sandwich cake tin Ø 22 cm. Put the egg yolks
into the processor bowl fitted with the kneading
blade (or the metal blade). Add 110g sugar and
orange blossom water. Beat for 30 secs on
speed 3 / ❷ speed 1. Blend in the butter then
the sifted flour and cornflour giving 5 to 6 short
bursts using the *Pulse* button. Mix for 10 secs.
Put aside in a salad bowl
2. Wash the bowl, replace the kneading blade
with the whisk attachment (or the whipping
disk) and beat the egg whites to a firm stiff snow
on speed 5 / ❷ speed 2. Add 15g sugar halfway
through. Blend the egg whites into the mixture
very carefully. Pour the mixture into the
sandwich tin immediately and bake for 30 mins.
Leave to cool before turning out.
3. During this time wash the strawberries. Hull
and halve them. Beat the white cream cheese with
the whisk on speed 1 to smoothen and blend in
the sugar and the orange blossom water.
4. When the cake is completely cool, cut it
through its width to obtain 2 circles. Melt the
redcurrant jelly. Brush the jelly over the circle to
be used as the cake base. Next cover the surface
with the halved strawberries and cover with half
of the white cream cheese. Place the second circle
of sponge on top of the first and coat the top with
the jelly, then the rest of the white cream cheese.
To decorate arrange the strawberries so that
they slighly overlap. Glaze the fruit and the
sides of the cake with the melted jelly. Decorate
the sides of the cake with almonds.

All chocolate cake

SERVES 6

200g plain cooking chocolate,
125g butter, 125g sugar, 60g flour
4 eggs, 10g butter to grease tin

PREPARATION : 15 mins
COOKING TIME : 40 mins

1. Grease and flour a Ø 22 cm cake tin.
Preheat the oven at 160°C (Gas Mark 5-6)).
Break the chocolate into pieces and melt over
a bain-marie (or in the microwave) with
2 tablespoons of water. Remove from heat,
add butter knobs and blend until the mixture
is smooth. Leave to cool.
2. Put the egg yolks and 100g sugar in the
processor bowl fitted with the whisk
attachment. Mix on speed 2 for 30 secs, add the
melted chocolate and blend the flour using the
Pulse button. Mix well.
3. Wash the bowl, the whisk and beat the egg
whites to a stiff snow on speed 5. After 1 mins
30 add 25g sugar and beat for a further 10 secs.
4. Fold the egg whites carefully into the
mixture in 3 goes. Pour the mixture into the tin
and bake for 40 to 45 mins. Turn out on to a
cooling rack.
▷ *You can also use the kneading blade (or the
metal blade).*

Madeira cake

5 eggs, 250g sugar
Grated peel of a large lemon
250g flour
250g butter at room temperature
1 sachet baking powder

1. Grease and flour a round cake tin Ø 25 cm.
Preheat the oven at 200°C (Gas Mark 6-7).
Break the egg into the bowl of the processor
fitted with the kneading blade (or the metal
blade), add sugar and lemon peel.
Set on speed 3 / ② on 1 and blend for 30 secs.
Add the sifted flour, baking powder and diced
butter. Start the processor on speed 2 /
② speed 1 and blend until the mixture is
smooth and even.
2. Pour the mixture into the cake tin and bake
in the oven for 1 hour. To see if it is ready,
pierce the centre of the cake with a clean blade.
If it comes out clean, the cake is ready. Turn the
cake out to cool on a wire cooling rack.

LEMON GLAZING : gradually add 2 tablespoons of lemon juice to 120g icing sugar,
stirring with a fork to obtain a very smooth
mixture. Pour the glazing over the cooled cake
and smoothen with a spatula. Leave to harden.

MARBLE CAKE : replace the lemon peel with
the inside of a vanilla pod. Pour two thirds of
the mixture into the cake tin in an even layer.
Sift 20g cocoa into the rest of the mixture in the
processor bowl. Restart the appliance until the
mixture is the same colour all over. Lift it out
with a spoon and spread evenly over the clear
mixture. With a fork trace a spiral pattern
across the layers to create a marble effect. Put
the tin into the oven and bake for 1 hour.

Blending

1. Pound cake : select speed 3 / ② speed 1.
Mix the eggs and the sugar.

2. Then add the softened butter, flour and the
baking powder...

3... then turn up gradually to 4 to obtain a
smooth and even mixture. If you are preparing
a large quantity of mixture at a time use speed
5 / ② speed 2.

Sponge cake

SERVES 4 TO 6

170g self raising flour
1 heaped teaspoon baking powder
170g butter (room temperature), 170g sugar
3 eggs size 3 (60 to 65g)
2 tablespoons of milk (optional)

PREPARATION : 10 mins
COOKING TIME : 30 mins

1. Grease a baking tin Ø 20 cm and dust with flour. Sieve the flour with the baking powder.
2. Cut the butter into knobs and put it with the sugar into the processor bowl fitted with the kneading blade (or the metal blade). Set the speed on 3 / ❷ speed 1 and mix for 30 secs in order to obtain a cream, then add the eggs one by one through the feeder tube leaving the processor on.
3. Preheat the oven at 175°C (Gas Mark 5-6). Gradually blend in the flour, leaving the processor on. If the mixture is too thick add some milk.
4. When the mixture is smooth pour it into the tin and bake the cake for 30 mins.

Trifle

SERVES 4 TO 6

300g sponge cake
(about half of the above cake)
3 tablespoons raspberry jam,
250g raspberries, 50ml sherry
Custard
250ml milk, 3 egg yolks, 40g caster sugar
1 level teaspoon cornflour,
250 ml fresh cream (double cream),
1 tablespoon grilled trimmed almonds,

PREPARATION : 15 mins
COOKING TIME : 8 mins

1. Prepare the custard as indicated on page 47. Add cornflour when you beat the egg yolks with the sugar. Let it cool.
2. Break the cake in pieces and spread a little jam on each piece. Place them in a large glass bowl and sprinkle the raspberries and sherry over them. Cover with custard.
3. Whip the cream with the whisk attachment (or the whipping disk) at speed 4 / ❷ speed 1 and spread it on top of the mixture. Cover and refrigerate for at least 3 hours. Before serving decorate with the grilled trimmed almonds.

Scones

FOR 10 SCONES

250g flour
1 tablespoon baking powder
1 pinch salt, 50g butter at room temperature
100ml milk, 1 egg

PREPARATION : 10 mins
COOKING TIME : 15 mins

1. Put the sifted flour, salt and the baking powder into the bowl fitted with the kneading blade (or the metal blade). Set the speed on 3 / ❷ speed 1 and mix. Pour the milk gradually through the feeder tube and mix to a soft dough.
2. Preheat the oven at 200°C (Gas Mark 6-7). Shape the dough into a ball and roll it out on a floured pastry board to a thickness of about 1.5 cm. With a Ø 6 cm pastry cutter cut out as many scone shapes as you can, then gather up the excess dough to make a ball and repeat until you have used it all.
3. Place the scones on a greased baking sheet and bake for about 15 mins. Take out of the oven and put them on a wire cooling rack. Serve warm or cooled with butter or jam.

Brownies

SERVES 4 TO 6

150g dark cooking chocolate
120g softened butter
200g sugar
3 eggs
1 levelled teaspoon baking powder
80g flour
100g walnuts

Preparation : 10 mins
Baking time : 35 mins

1. Grease and flour a 24 cm x 19 cm x 3 cm baking tin. Preheat the oven at 180°C (Gas Mark 6). Blend the butter and the sugar in the processor bowl fitted with the kneading blade (or the metal blade) on speed 3 / **2** speed 1 in order to obtain a creamy mixture.
2. Coarsely chop the walnuts using the mini-chopper (or the metal blade). Break the chocolate into pieces and melt in a bain-marie (or in the microwave) with 2 tablespoons of water. Add 1 tablespoon of the butter-sugar mixture and stir to smoothen. Leave to cool.
3. Put the eggs into the processor bowl fitted with the kneading blade and blend quickly. Add the chocolate then the sifted flour with the baking powder. Continue blending until you obtain a smooth texture. Finally add the nuts and mix using the *Pulse* button.
4. Transfer the mixture into the tin and bake for 35 mins. Turn out on to a wire rack and leave to cool.

Chopping small quantities

1. To chop nuts, almonds, chocolate ...in small quantities, use the mini-chopper. Select speed 3. To obtain coarsely chopped nuts, use the Pulse button in order to control the end result.

2. Depending on desired result : coarse chopping, fine chopping or powder, increase the speed and the chopping time.

Cheesecake

SERVES 6

Pastry
200g flour
1 level teaspoon baking powder
50g sugar
1 egg
75g butter (at room temperature)
Filling
450g ricotta (cream cheese)
60g sugar, 3 eggs
1 sachet vanilla sugar
15g cornflour
1 tablespoon grated lemon peel

PREPARATION : 15 mins
COOKING TIME : 1 hour - Plan before

1. Pour the sifted flour with the baking powder in the processor bowl fitted with the kneading blade (or the metal blade). Add the egg and sugar. Set on speed 2 / ❷ speed 1 and start to mix. Add the butter and knead on speed 4 / ❷ speed 1 to quickly obtain a smooth mixture (add some water if necessary). Leave to cool 15 mins in the refrigerator.
2. Preheat the oven at 180°C (Gas Mark 6). Grease and flour a Ø 22 cm baking tin. Spread the pastry and fill the tin.
3. Pour the ricotta in the processor bowl fitted with the kneading blade. Add sugar, vanilla, the egg yolks, cornflour and the lemon peel. Mix on speed 3 / ❷ speed 1. Clean the bowl and beat the egg whites to a stiff snow on speed 5 / ❷ speed 1 with the whisk attachment (or the whipping disk). Fold the egg whites carefully into the previous mixture.
4. Pour the mixture on top of the cheesecake base and bake for 45 mins. Leave the cake to cool in the tin before turning out.

▷ *You can also add candied or dried fruit to the cream cheese mixture.*

Fruit cake

SERVES 6 TO 8

90g sultanas
50g currants
50g candied lemon and orange
125g softened butter
100g sugar, 3 eggs
250 g sifted flour
1 sachet baking powder
5 tablespoons milk

PREPARATION : 10 mins
COOKING TIME : 1 h 15 mins

1. Preheat the oven at 180°C (Gas Mark at 6). Grease and flour a loaf tin 24 cm x 10 cm x 7 cm. With the mini-chopper chop the candied fruit peel coarsely using the *Pulse button*. Put into a bowl with the currants, sultanas and a tablespoon of flour. Mix and put aside.
2. Fit the kneading blade on the processor (or the metal blade) put the butter and sugar in the bowl and blend for 20 secs at speed 3 / ❷ speed 1. Add the eggs one at a time through the feeder tube then the milk. Stop the processor and pour in the flour with the baking powder. Start mixing at speed 1 to get a smooth mixture.
3. Mix in the fruit in short bursts at first, then for 10 secs on speed 4 / ❷ speed 1 (if using the metal blade, in short bursts only). Pour the mixture into the loaf tin and bake for 1 h 15 mins. Turn out on to a cooling rack.

▷ *You can also soak the currants and sultanas in a little rum.*

RECIPE INDEX

Imprimé en France   Aubin Imprimeur
                         LIGUGÉ, POITIERS